BEATRIX ATTITUDES AND ENTHUSIASMS

BEATRIX POTTER STUDIES VI
Papers presented at
The Beatrix Potter Society Conference
Ambleside, England, July 1994

Text © 1995 Selwyn Goodacre, Robert Leeson, Victoria Slowe,
Joyce Irene Whalley, Michael Wilson

Copyright in this compilation
© 1995 The Beatrix Potter Society

Edited by Enid Bassom, Rowena Knox and Irene Whalley,
with the assistance of Isobel Joseph

TITLE PAGE ILLUSTRATION
Beatrix Potter, photographed by Rupert Potter

FRONT COVER ILLUSTRATION
Mrs Tiggy-winkle dips shirt-fronts into the starch,
from *The Tale of Mrs Tiggy-Winkle*, 1905

BACK COVER ILLUSTRATION
Mrs Tittlemouse in her little box bed,
from *The Tale of Mrs Tittlemouse*, 1910

Produced by Sue Coley

ISBN 1 869980 10 7

Printed by Redwood Books Ltd, Trowbridge, Wiltshire

Contents

ACKNOWLEDGEMENTS FOR ILLUSTRATIONS

The Beatrix Potter Society is grateful to the following for permission to reproduce illustrations:

P.J. Buxton: Dunkeld Cathedral (p. 20)

City of Bristol Museum & Art Gallery: *The Mermaid*, Lord Leighton (p. 45), © City of Bristol Museum and Art Gallery

Dulwich Picture Gallery: *Mrs Siddons as the Tragic Muse*, Sir Joshua Reynolds (p. 47), by permission of the Governors of the Dulwich Picture Gallery

Manchester City Art Gallery: *Prince Arthur and Hubert*, W.F. Yeames (p. 43), *The Hireling Shepherd*, W. Holman Hunt (p. 52), © Manchester City Art Gallery,

Perth Museum & Art Gallery: Charlie Macintosh in about 1898 (p. 74)

Pope Family Trust: *Private View at the Royal Academy*, W.P. Frith (p. 40–41)

Rosalind Rawnsley: Canon Rawnsley with Beatrix Potter (p. 37)

The Tate Gallery: *Christ in the House of his Parents*, J.E. Millais (p. 53), *King Cophetua and the Beggar Maid*, E.C. Burne Jones (p. 53), *Love Locked Out*, A.L. Merritt (p. 54), by permission of the Tate Gallery

Torquay Museum: Beatrix Potter at Torquay (page 76)

Frederick Warne & Co: Watercolour for *The Tale of Mrs Tiggy-Winkle* (front cover), © F. Warne & Co, 1905, 1987; watercolour for *The Tale of Mrs Tittlemouse* (back cover, p. 8), © F. Warne & Co, 1910, 1987; watercolour for *The Tale of Jemima Puddle-Duck* (p. 12), © F. Warne & Co, 1908, 1987; line drawing and watercolour for *The Tale of Samuel Whiskers* (p. 13, p. 64), © F. Warne & Co, 1908, 1987; watercolour for *The Tale of Johnny Town-Mouse* (p. 15), © F. Warne & Co, 1918, 1987; The invitation to Sir Isaac Newton, from the Linder Bequest, Victoria & Albert Museum (p. 16), © F. Warne & Co, 1985; Photograph of William Ewart Gladstone by Rupert Potter, from the Linder Bequest, Victoria & Albert Museum (p. 26), courtesy Warne Archive; Election Poster, from the Linder Bequest, Victoria & Albert Museum (p. 34), © F. Warne & Co, 1987; watercolour from *The Tale of Peter Rabbit* (p. 54), © F. Warne & Co, 1902, 1987; Brideswaine from the Linder Bequest, Victoria & Albert Museum, © F. Warne & Co,1985; drawing for *The Tale of the Pie and the Patty-Pan* (p. 60), © F. Warne & Co, 1905, 1987; sketch for *Cecily Parsley's Nursery Rhymes* from the Linder Bequest, Victoria & Albert Museum (page 61), © F. Warne & Co, 1985; Mary Ellen by the fire from *The Fairy Caravan* (page 63), © F. Warne & Co, 1929; watercolour for *The Tale of Mr Tod* (p. 68), © F. Warne & Co, 1912, 1987; sketch of Lucie's farm from the Linder Bequest, Victoria & Albert Museum (p. 70), © F. Warne & Co, 1987; watercolour for *The Tale of Tom Kitten* (p. 77), © F. Warne & Co, 1907, 1987; drawing for *The Tale of Ginger & Pickles* (p. 78), © F. Warne & Co, 1910, 1987; drawing for the privately printed edition of *The Tale of Peter Rabbit* (page 79), © F. Warne & Co, 1987.

The illustration on the title page is © The Beatrix Potter Society, 1994

Introduction

EVERY alternate year since 1984 the Beatrix Potter Society has held an International Study Conference in the Lake District or in Scotland. These Conferences have been attended by members from all parts of the United Kingdom and from as far away as the United States, Australia and Japan. The proportion of the membership who can actually attend these Conferences is small, and therefore the Society has always followed a policy of publishing the proceedings under the title *Beatrix Potter Studies*.

The first Conference, held in Ambleside in 1984, was general in content, but since then each one has been concerned with a special theme or themes. The subject for the 1992 Conference was a detailed consideration of Beatrix Potter's little books. In 1994, however, attention was focused on Beatrix herself, with a Conference title of 'Beatrix Potter's attitudes and enthusiasms'. This enabled the speakers to consider Beatrix less from a biographical point of view (such as had been attempted in 1990 with 'Beatrix Potter and Mrs Heelis') but rather to look further into the complexities of her character based on her attitudes and her enthusiasms.

As always when transferring the spoken word to the printed page a certain amount of editing has been necessary. But, as in previous *Studies*, the editors have not attempted to bring uniformity or formality to talks originally given in the informal atmosphere of the Conference itself. The Beatrix Potter Society has always been gratified by the range of interests of the speakers who have accepted invitations to speak at the Conferences, and by the high standard of the talks themselves, and 1994 was no exception. What has become apparent as these talks were prepared for publication was the importance to most of the speakers of Beatrix Potter's own *Journal* as a source of information – and indeed inspiration. While her letters and her little books all played their part in these talks, it is surely Beatrix's *Journal* which remains the supreme source book and we ignore it at our peril.

Notes on the Contributors

Selwyn Goodacre is Senior Partner in a semi-rural General Medical practice in south Derbyshire. He grew up in the Yorkshire Dales and studied medicine at Birmingham University. He pursues an interest in minor surgery and has written a number of articles on the subject. He began collecting the works of Lewis Carroll as a teenager, and went on to collect Beatrix Potter piracies and 'continuations', also the works of Robert Bloomfield, the nineteenth-century pastoral poet, and Edmund Gosse, the literary critic. However, his chief interest remains the collection and study of classic children's literature. He currently edits the *Journal* of the Lewis Carroll Society.

Robert Leeson is a writer, journalist and critic. He is the author of more than fifty children's books, as well as plays and serials for radio and theatre; also adult social and industrial history studies, and works of literary criticism, including *Reading and Righting*, an assessment of children's literature past and present. In 1985 he received the Eleanor Farjeon Award for services to children's literature, encouraging pupils in reading and creative writing in over six hundred schools, and raising funds for schools and libraries in the Third World. He was Treasurer of the British Section of the International Board on Books for Young People, 1979–90, and Chairman of the Writers' Guild of Great Britain 1985–86. In 1994 he gave the Linder Memorial Lecture for the Beatrix Potter Society.

Vicky Slowe was Director of the Abbot Hall Art Gallery and The Museum of Lakeland Life and Industry, Kendal, from 1986 until 1993. She attributes her interest in the traditional farmhouses and oak furniture of the Lake District to a mixture of nature and nurture. She was taught to read using Beatrix Potter's little books as primers. Raised on a farm in Hawkshead, she was quick to appreciate the factual accuracy of both the landscape and the domestic 'sets' for the tales. Academic research into local vernacular architecture began while she was still at school and has continued through her subsequent career as a museum curator, specialising in the fine and decorative arts, with particular interest in landscape appreciation. She is directly associated with the Windermere ferry to Hill Top footpath scheme, and is curatorial advisor to the Windermere Steamboat Museum and to Heron

Corn Mill, Beetham, among others. She is a founder member of the Arthur Ransome Society. Vicky Slowe is currently Project Director at the Ruskin Museum, Coniston, leading a major development scheme.

Irene Whalley was for many years on the staff of the National Art Library, Victoria and Albert Museum, where she was responsible for manuscripts and rare books. The latter included a collection of early children's books and the Leslie Linder Bequest of Beatrix Potter material. She is the author of a number of books and articles on early children's book illustration, the history of calligraphy, and Beatrix Potter. She has been involved in Beatrix Potter exhibitions at the Victoria and Albert Museum, the Grey Art Gallery, New York, and other American galleries, the Tate Gallery, London, and in Wales; she also produced for Japan 'The Enchanted World of Peter Rabbit and Winnie-the-Pooh'. She is a founder member of the Beatrix Potter Society and has served on its committee since its inception.

Michael Wilson's school years were spent in Westmorland, in the shadow of the Pennines, and it was here that his abiding interest in Beatrix Potter was first aroused. He graduated from Durham University and in 1958 went to London to join the staff of the Victoria and Albert Museum, where he remained until his retirement in 1990. For most of that time he worked in the National Art Library (where he was a colleague of Irene Whalley and Anne Hobbs) and he retired as Chief Cataloguer. He has followed a parallel career as a writer and lecturer, and has published a number of articles and books on various aspects of the arts. His two most recent books have been biographies: one of the eighteenth century architect and decorator William Kent, and the other about seventeenth-century Nicholas Lanier, first Master of the King's Music and also one of the first great art collectors and connoisseurs. In 1995 he gave the Linder Memorial Lecture for the Beatrix Potter Society.

These biographies have been edited from accounts supplied by the contributors themselves.

Mrs Tittlemouse and Mr Jackson: 'He sat such
a while that he had to be asked if he would take
some dinner?'

Beatrix Potter as Observer and Recorder of the Social Scene

JOYCE IRENE WHALLEY

THE ARTICLE which follows was of course originally given as a *talk* at the Beatrix Potter Society's Sixth International Study Conference – this is true of all the other articles printed here. Usually the main problem the author encounters when preparing a talk for printing is that the visual material, in the form of slides, is no longer available to supplement the text, and at best the published version has to make do with a small selection of illustrations. But my problem was a different one, since my 'illustrations' were verbal not visual, and for these there is no suitable substitution. As I gave the first part of my talk I was able to emphasise the points I was making by changing my own voice, its emphasis and pronunciation, however inadequately this was done. I cannot do this on the printed page, except by, in some cases, using phonetic spelling, as then I would be tampering with my text. It is therefore very difficult to convey some of the ideas inherent in this article, especially to overseas readers whose perception of the English class system is probably non-existent, and whose own pronunciation of English is quite different. Nevertheless I hope that something of Beatrix Potter's powers of observation will come across, showing how she noted the differences in speech and pronunciation, and in forms of address, among the various classes of society in the late nineteenth and early twentieth centuries.

My other problem was quite different. When I gave this talk I was able to illustrate various aspects of it with long passages from Beatrix Potter's *Journal*, read for me by fellow Society member Veronica Hickie. To print such long passages in this article would be quite inappropriate, and I can therefore only give a summary of the main drift of the paragraphs quoted and refer the reader to the full passage in the *Journal* itself.

With someone as long-lived as Beatrix Potter, the amount of material at my disposal was overwhelming when it had to be compressed into a comparatively short talk, and I therefore made a decision at the beginning of my study that I would confine my attention to 'Beatrix Potter', and ignore her later life as 'Mrs Heelis'. I have concentrated on the woman who was the writer and artist rather than the one who was the wife, countrywoman and farmer. I have also had to avoid trespassing on other subjects to be discussed in this Conference – her art, politics and humour, which in my main sources are greatly intermingled. These sources are the little books themselves, the early letters, and of course the *Journal*.

I am going to start my talk with a commercial – at least it would be if the item concerned was not now out of print. More than twenty years ago I was asked to write a book on the illustration of early children's books. Under the title *Cobwebs to catch flies: illustrated books for the nursery and schoolroom, 1700–1900*, it was published in this country by Paul Elek and in the United States by the University of California Press. I based the work on the collections of the Victoria and Albert Museum where I was then employed. Since I believe that a good illustrated book is the marriage of text and pictures, I read all the books that I discussed – both the authors' prefaces and the texts themselves. The authors' introductions told me more or less what I expected to find there, but what I did discover as I read the texts of these eighteenth and nineteenth century books intended for use by young children in the home, was a wonderful source of social behaviour and of contemporary living conditions – all of course provided quite incidentally. I cannot, in a talk on Beatrix Potter, go into details, but I will quote just a couple of examples to show what I mean.

One of the chapters in my book was devoted to the study of early reading books for children. In these I frequently found examples of conversation, often in words of one, two or three syllables, increasing in difficulty with the age of the child. But in spite of the limitations thus imposed, these surely were echoes of real conversations between adults and children – the echoes of long-ago speech. I learnt useful facts too, such as that 'butter is not good for little boys' – indeed their main diet seems to have been bread and milk as far as I could see! In a book by Maria Edgeworth called *Early Lessons* I came across another kind of social revelation. Little Frank has asked his father some simple question, the answer to which we know will take up several pages – that was the sort of didactic reading offered to the child in the late eighteenth and early nineteenth century. But before he begins his reply, the father sends little Frank into his study to bring him something – a ruler or a thermometer, I forget which. What he says to the child is revealing: 'It is on the desk in my study. You are a big boy now, Frank, and are not afraid to go by yourself in the dark.' Immediately I saw in a flash what it was like even in a wealthy household, where to leave the family living-room meant a plunge into darkness and cold, and where life tended to be lived co-operatively in one room for these very reasons.

All this may seem a long way from Beatrix Potter, but it was these sorts of points that I kept in mind as I studied my present theme. First, could we trace 'recordings' of actual speech and conversation, especially in the little books, and then, could we learn something of contemporary ways of life from incidental comments or actual descriptions? My interest in the whole field of Beatrix Potter as a social observer and recorder had been further stimulated by an experience which took place some years ago when we were planning our first Post-Conference Tour of the Scottish Borders. We had decided to take the group to Berwick-on-Tweed, and to show them the fortifications and the old Barracks. Of course we went there ourselves first, and while in the Barracks, now also a museum, we went into the various exhibitions then on show. One was something to do with women's labour in the late nineteenth century. There were blown-up photographs showing groups of 'bondagers', as they were called, going along the roads or working in the fields, always in groups as they went from employer to employer seeking work. And there was even exhibited an actual surviving bonnet of the kind that the bondagers were wearing in the pictures. Now this was really exciting. By then we knew the Borders part of Beatrix Potter's *Journal* almost by heart, and we remembered very well her comments, so relevant to what we were seeing. On 1 August 1894 Beatrix writes, 'At one point we overtook a troop of farm labourers . . . coming away from hoeing turnips . . . . The women are dark and on the whole good-looking . . . . Their dress in the fields is in this wise peculiar, that it is impossible to say without peeping under their sun-bonnets and pink hand-kerchiefs whether it is an old woman or a young girl. My father was rather taken aback, on passing the time of day to one whom we overtook, to see her turn round the face of a child.' Looking at the large bonnet in the case before us, and at the photographs of just such a scene, we could indeed see the problem.

It was all these things about which I have just spoken that led me on to look for yet more clues to the social scene, in all its aspects, in Beatrix Potter's writings. If we take the little books to start with, there are two different approaches. There are times when the characters are actually speaking to each other, or to themselves; and there are times when the story itself calls for a certain kind of social behaviour, as in the *The Tale of The Pie and The Patty-Pan*. Now one of the interesting things that I have learnt from my study of early children's books is that there is nearly always a certain time-lag in them, which is far less likely to be found in adult books. Children's books are written and illustrated by adults – how old was Beatrix when she wrote her first book? And adults tend to forget, unless they live in a child-orientated

11

circle, that speech, customs and fashion have moved on since their own day as children. To give one example in the field of illustration: little boys and girls were still shown wearing short trousers or skirts in books long after they were in fact both wearing jeans and T-shirts. In dating older books it is often possible to do so from the costumes shown in the illustrations, but the wary bibliographer knows that in those for children's books one has to watch out for this time-lag. So when we read in Beatrix Potter's books of forms of behaviour, or conversations, the chances are that we are reading recollections of Beatrix's own childhood ways, rather than those of children contemporary with the time when she was writing. And indeed a study of the texts will confirm this rather old-fashioned speech and formality, which was more characteristic of the late nineteenth century than of the early twentieth century, when Beatrix's books were being published.

Let us start then with some actual examples of conversation to be found in the little books. Beatrix Potter had an ear finely tuned to speech – of all kinds. We can tell this from her use of speech in the little books, where she carefully distinguishes between that of polite conversation among the upper-class animals, and the more casual speech of the workers. Look at *The Tale of Jemima Puddle-Duck*: in the farmyard Rebeccah Puddle-duck says chattily, 'I have not the patience to sit on a nest for twenty-eight days; and no more have you, Jemima. You would let them go cold; you know you would!' But the

'Madam, I beg you not to trouble yourself with
a bag.'

'We are discovered and interrupted, Anna Maria.'

elegantly dressed gentleman whom Jemima thought mighty civil, speaks quite differently, 'Madam, have you lost your way?'. We can almost see Rupert Potter raising his hat and saying those same words to a chance-met stranger. The fox's speech is always fairly formal: 'Madam, I beg you not to trouble yourself with a bag.' 'Before you commence your tedious sitting.' 'May I ask you to bring up some herbs from the farm-garden?' Here we surely have echoes of Potter family sentences, dimly remembered perhaps. Mrs Tittlemouse provides echoes too: 'I am not in the habit of letting lodgings; this is an intrusion!', says the tidy housekeeper. The big fat spider is clearly a tradesman calling: 'Beg pardon, is this not Miss Muffet's?'. The subtle difference is there if you have ears to hear it, but with the passing of time and changes in speech patterns, these social distinctions become less obvious. In the same book is surely another echo, perhaps of Mrs Potter this time: 'He sat such a while that he had to be asked if he would take some dinner?' – you can almost hear Mrs Potter's complaining voice. The conversation between the two abandoned wives in *The Tale of Timmy Tiptoes* also has its formal overtones, as when the two ladies meet for the first time: 'I am sure I beg your pardon; I did not know that anybody lived here.'

Mrs Tiggy-winkle offers the obvious example of servant speech, with her constant 'If you please'm' in answer to all Lucie's questions, and in other phrases like 'Most terrible particular'. Contrasts appear again in *The Tale of Samuel Whiskers*. Here Beatrix is undoubtedly echoing local Cumbrian speech rather than that of her London home, when she makes Mrs Tabitha Twitchett say 'Come in, Cousin Ribby, come in, and sit ye down!'. But Samuel Whiskers himself is undoubtedly a gentleman rogue, a cad of the old school, and his speech is quite different: 'Will not the string be very indigestible, Anna Maria?'. 'We are discovered and interrupted, Anna Maria; let us collect our property – and other people's – and depart at once.' 'But I am persuaded that the knots would have proved indigestible, whatever you may urge to the contrary.' This is much more the speech of educated people, however fallen their status!

I hope I have said enough here for you all to go on looking for further examples of conversation from the Potter household in the little books for yourselves. I now want to look at the books from the point of view of social behaviour. See how the squirrels make formal application to Old Mr Brown for permission to pick his nuts: 'Old Mr Brown, will you favour us with permission to gather nuts upon your island?'. *The Tale of The Pie and The Patty-Pan* is also full of formal 'company' manners. Polite letters are exchanged between host and guest even though they live so near. And when Duchess had written 'I hope it isn't mouse?', she felt that it did not look quite polite, so scratched it out: as it was to be a party, she decided she would have to eat it, even if it *were* mouse. When the two animals met in the village during the day 'they only bowed to one another; they did not speak, because they were going to have a party'. All this carries distant echoes of the formality obtaining in Beatrix's own childhood – though one does wonder if she was ever allowed to go to parties. Again in this book we see the social niceties which have now probably passed away: 'Is Mrs Ribston at home?' 'Come in! and how do you do, my dear Duchess?' cried Ribby. 'I hope I see you well?' But even today a guest may arrive, like Duchess, with a bunch of flowers for her hostess, so not everything has changed.

The Tale of Johnny Town-Mouse is very much a book of manners, though it also surely contains echoes of Potter family life. Beatrix writes: 'The family had gone to the sea-side for Easter; the cook was doing spring cleaning, on board wages, with particular instructions to clear out the mice' – very much the Potter family routine in the days before Beatrix's marriage! Then there is the social round. Timmy Willie drops into the dinner party – quite literally – ' "Who in the world is this?", inquired Johnny Town-mouse. But after the first exclamation of surprise he instantly recovered his manners. With the utmost politeness he introduced Timmy Willie to nine other mice, all with long tails and white neck-ties'. These town mice were far too well-bred to make personal remarks, even though they noticed that Timmy Willie's tail was shorter than theirs. 'The dinner was of eight courses; not much of anything, but truly elegant.' Poor Timmy Willie was so anxious to behave with company manners, and we wonder if Beatrix was recalling her own childhood experiences in company, and the instructions given to her before she was presented to her mother's callers. The more we look into the little books the more we find that which it suits us to find. I have only picked on a few examples here to quote in detail, but there are more instances to be discovered by the careful seeker.

Johnny Town-mouse dines with Timmy Willie
and friends: 'The dinner was of eight courses;
not much of anything, but truly elegant.'

This same sort of evidence can also be seen in the letters, especially in those to children, and in the miniature letters in particular. Thanks to Judy Taylor's books we now have a wealth of these to choose from. I am just going to quote a few examples here, since we can all find more for ourselves. But I cannot resist including a few passages which show how the letters written by some of the characters from the little books continue to convey distinct social nuances, indicative of their station in life. Notice for example the way in which the miniature letters begin and end – Beatrix is perhaps recalling echoes of the past here. Squirrel Nutkin writes to Old Mr Brown 'Sir, I should esteem it a favour if you would let me have back my tail', signing himself 'Yrs. truly'. Later he writes 'Dear Sir, I should be extremely obliged' and signs himself 'Yrs. respectifully' [sic]. Then there is the formal dinner invitation, of the kind with which Beatrix must have been very familiar in her early life: 'Mr Alderman Ptolemy Tortoise request[s] the pleasure of Sir Isaac Newton's company at dinner'. A change of scene and a change of class: Tom Thumb writes to Miss Lucinda Doll as 'Honoured Madam', and ends, in true tradesman fashion 'Yr obedient humble servant, Thomas Thumb'. But Lucinda Doll, house-owner, writes in lofty fashion to Mrs Tom Thumb: 'Miss Lucinda Doll will require Hunca Munca to come for the whole day on Saturday' – echoes of Mrs Potter again? Look for yourselves, there are plenty more of these letters, so full of unconscious period charm, and carrying overtones of Beatrix's youth.

But Beatrix Potter was more than just a translator of the social scene into books. She was also, in her letters and *Journal*, a fine recorder of what she saw

15

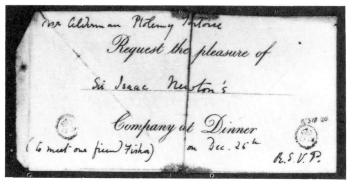

A formal invitation to dinner from Alderman Ptolemy
Tortoise to Sir Isaac Newton

as she went about the country in her parents' wake, with her eyes and ears wide open. The *Journal* is of course the most marvellous source book and every re-reading brings out something new. But first let us see what we can discover in it about the more intimate aspects of Potter family life. In Beatrix's youth there were no means of recording speech, so how did the Potters actually talk? We get just one good clue from the entry for 25 July 1884: 'Bertram came home from school .... He seems very well, only rather inclined to say "pāth, grāss" (i.e. 'parth' and 'grarss').' Now the implication is that this is not what the Potters usually said. They must still have retained in London their original northern accent and said 'grăss' and 'păth' (with a short 'a'). This is only one of a number of indications that although the Potters lived a well-to-do *London* life, they were still conscious of being outsiders, which was emphasised by the fact that they were also Unitarians and not members of the established Church. I wonder if it was this sense of never quite belonging that affected Mrs Potter's behaviour? There is also a nice touch from Beatrix in the *Journal* which links up with the passage I have already quoted from *The Tale of Johnny Town-Mouse*, about spring cleaning. It is dated April 1883: 'Bother spring cleaning! I could have put my finger in the dark on most books in the cupboard in the drawing room. I have stared at them for hours, though hardly opened any, and when I went there the other day, I couldn't believe my eyes, I took out several books and they all came wrong.' Don't we all know that feeling after a good tidy-up!

What does Beatrix tell us about other members of the family? On 18 March 1885 she writes that she went with papa and mama and Edith to the theatre. She thought the drive there the most interesting part of the affair: 'We had to fetch papa from the Athenaeum [Club], but when we got to Buckingham Palace Road Her Majesty was having a Drawing-Room. We saw the Duchess of Westminster and such grand carriages, and coming home, the Beefeaters marching. We stuck for about half an hour [traffic jams even then!], and after all had to go back round by Westminster, where all the great coaches were drinking at the inns. Of course papa was in a great state thinking we had had a carriage accident.' And on 20 March she writes: 'went to an exhibition of Art which is being held for Charity in Devonshire House, Belgrave Square [one of the great noblemen's town houses]. My father always goes to Exhibitions of that kind because he is curious to see the insides of great houses'.

Now for a few other domestic scenes, this time to do with troublesome neighbours. Again on 20 March Beatrix writes: 'We had an awful to-do with the Saunders' kitchen chimney, badly on fire for the second time since Xmas. It is very unpleasant, crowd in road, police, showers of sparks on both roofs, high wind, 10 o'clock at night, sweep in bed, and criers of battles on the top of all. They are very careless, and used to continually set it on fire at No.3, which they denied flat, but one day the Silbers' butler bounced into their kitchen and found it full of burnt smoke.' But that was not the worst. In May of the same year 1885, there was another exciting incident: 'Last Saturday night, between twelve and one, being moonlight, the neighbourhood was awakened by a female who need not fear to walk the streets by night, seeing that in seven minutes she can summon as many 'Bull's-Eyes' [police, so-called from the lanterns they carried] from a radius of half a mile. This presumed distressed female in the back lane, suddenly set up piercing and continuous shrieking with strangely powerful lungs. My father woke suddenly, bounced out of bed to the window, and acted upon by the sudden rising and sympathetic emotion, exclaimed "Dear me, I feel faint", and bounced into bed again, while mamma humped out at the other side. Meanwhile the screaming was something awful, and all the windows along the row were opened, and police were hurrying up from distant beats. They all enquired in chorus "What's the matter, what's the matter, do be quiet and tell us my dear!"'. Whereat the distressed female screamed louder for the course of five minutes.' The whole of this disturbance in the quiet Kensington neighbourhood was obviously relished by Beatrix and her description brings the scene vividly before us. The 'victim' turned out to be a drunken servant from a nearby house, but it certainly made a good story.

The Potters always liked to be in the fashion, but were nearly caught out over the local celebrations of Queen Victoria's Jubilee in 1887 ('the lower classes pronounce it Jew *billy*'). 'On Monday we were very busy arranging our fairy lights, on each of the nine front window sills, seven red in each length, five white above and three blue at the top. The Square are mostly hanging bottles and paper lanterns, the latter very pretty but most unsafe. After lunch mamma and I were greatly excited to see the Westgarths set out three flags, we having none. An anxious watch was kept on our neighbour and enemy Mr Saunders. Nothing happened during the afternoon, but at tea, a small crowd was noticed. Mr Saunders was letting down a rope with six small banners attached, from the top floor window. We hurried out in a cab and procured an immense Union Jack at a fancy price. There was not a yard of Turkey red to be had at any price. I wish we had had an idea that flags would be so general. Three quarters of the houses have them, there is only one in this square without.' But nevertheless, the Potters' flag was not ideal, for on 21 June she writes, 'There is a most awful wind this afternoon, but it makes it cooler. Our flag is a perfect nuisance for rolling up.' Still, they *were* in the swim!

The Potters of course lived mostly in London – at least, they lived there at the socially 'proper' time, just as they went into the country at the 'proper' time, namely in the spring, when the house was cleaned through, and for three months every summer. As to London, Beatrix notes throughout the early part of her *Journal* how the area around her home was gradually being developed. New wooden pavements were laid, trees were chopped down and roads were cut across fields (yes, there were even orchards in that part of London then). She looks at the new houses going up: 'The Dutch houses are mostly finished. Mr Gilbert's is said to contain twenty-six bedrooms with a bath-room to each (fancy twenty-six burst water-pipes). It is a very handsome house with its marble court, but I should doubt the comfort of the little latticed-windows' – there spoke the practical Beatrix. 'If ever I had a house', she wrote in 1884, 'I would have old furniture, oak in the dining room, and Chippendale in the drawing room. It is not as expensive as modern furniture, and incomparably handsomer and better made.'

I will end this section of my talk with an extract from the *Journal*, which, in my opinion, links together a number of the social aspects that I have spoken about so far: Beatrix's relationship with her parents, her acute observation of her surroundings, and her subsequent recording and interpretation of what she had seen and the people she had met. On 1 February 1886 she made an expedition which she described in great detail, but unfortunately the long passage read at the Conference cannot be included in full here, and I can only refer the reader to the *Journal* entry for 1 February 1886, in which Beatrix describes this visit with her mother to Lady Eastlake, 'to fetch a drawing by one of her nieces which she had persuaded my father to buy'. Beatrix confessed to being rather curious to see Lady Eastlake, but her mother was reluctant 'according to her the old lady was a perfect dragon'. 'The Square itself seemed old-fashioned, substantial and genteel, perhaps a trifle passé on a foggy day, but this afternoon the low winter sun slanted pleasantly between the chimney-tops, through the leafless plane trees, on the cheerful sparrows airing themselves along the grooves in the masonry, and also showed up the thick ancient dust upon the window panes.' She notes the outside and the inside of the house, and then describes the butler who admitted them and who 'hurried up the steep staircase like a beetle. He turned out his feet at right angles; they were very large, or rather his shiny shoes were, I could not make out his feet, they were all knobs. I was very much impressed by them as he went up before, two steps at a time.' She describes in detail the room into which they were then admitted, and the dress and appearance of Lady Eastlake. One feels that while Mrs Potter made heavy polite conversation, Beatrix was sitting silently noting all this, ready to record it on her return. Her account covers nearly three pages of the printed *Journal*, and also contains scraps of the conversation, which she uses, as might a dramatist, to reveal aspects of Lady Eastlake's personality and character. When they rose to go ' "Will you ring the bell, my dear? pull it out a long way". Jonathan the little old man knocking and sticking in his head. "Will you take two supplements from the bottom of the heap and wrap up the drawing". John selected two whole sheets, though the drawing was small, laid them on, and, as no string appeared, held them on somewhat feebly, for *them* slipped off when he was half way down stairs. I noticed he descended two steps at a time as he had mounted.' Yet the whole visit had lasted only about twenty minutes!

I have quoted parts of that long passage because I think it gives us a very good picture of Beatrix's powers of observation, and her ability to recall and record such scenes at a later time. One feels that much of her young life was spent watching and listening, too shy to intrude her own opinions, especially at a time when it was definitely a case of children being seen and not heard. It was surely this acute awareness of the passing scene that made the keeping of the *Journal* so vital for her. She offers us numerous cameo portraits of the characters she meets, both of their physical appearance and of their behaviour. Here is a quick portrait of the general run of Cornish people based on her observations at Falmouth in 1892. 'The children are extremely pretty, but like the Welsh, it goes off. The women certainly are not on the whole, though intelligent and fresh-complexioned. The universal type is black or rusty, with crisp hair, women more black than men, and blue eyes very common with both shades .... As the men's faces become thinner through age, it is apparent that they have high cheek-bones. I notice with the red type, the nose is occasionally less straight, but always short. The women have singularly oval faces.' And here is a rather harsh one of arriving at Perth station after an overnight journey from London – which probably accounts for the tone! 'There was an extraordinary miscellaneous scramble in the first-class restaurant-room at Perth. A hard, hairy Scotcher opposite doing it thoroughly in five courses, porridge, salmon-cutlets, chops, ham and eggs and marmalade. Under my chair a black retriever and on my left a large man in knickerbockers, facing a particularly repulsive Scotch mother and young baby feeding on sops. All the company extremely dirty and the attendants inattentive.' Here is another Scottish picture, of Dunkeld Cathedral, from the same year. 'The portion of the Cathedral where public worship is held is walled out of the old building in an arbitrary ugly fashion. It is very plain inside, and down below intensely cold. We generally sit in the west gallery, the high old pews distressingly covered with hieroglyphics. They are open under the seat, and *non non quam* descends a peppermint, hop, hop, hop, from tier to tier. One looks down on the dusty tops of the sounding board, a rickety canopy carved somewhat to resemble the crown of St Giles Cathedral, but its effect is marred by being tipped forward as though it might fall on Mr Rutherford, earnest, pale and foxy-haired, with a pointed beard and decent Geneva bands.' It is surely the tiny details that she includes that make the scene so vivid, and convey a feeling of immediacy, which a general

Dunkeld Cathedral, Perthshire

description never does – here for example she notes the peppermint dropping down from the gallery – and also the dust to be seen from that height!

Another example of Beatrix's ability to recreate the social scene in the present tense can be found in her description of Mr Lowe the Postmaster at Birnam, near Dunkeld, where some of us will be going next week. 'What an aggravating old person Mr Lowe the post-master is! You go down in a hurry with two or three small affairs, say a postal order and three stamps. He says in a forbidding manner "let us do one thing first; *haveyougotapenny*?". He works out the change on his fingers, and after all has to carry on the halfpence to the next transaction which you work out for him as he has collapsed into a state of imbecility. "I *think* that's right" says he, regarding you sideways with evident suspicion. He is a fat, hunched old fellow, with little piggy eyes, a thick voice and wears a smoking-cap with a yellow tassel, and he has immense hands with which he slowly fumbles about for the stamps, which he keeps amongst the stationery in empty writing-paper boxes. He puts on wrong postage "shall we say tuppence?"(!) and will sauce anybody who is unprovided with small change; he wants reporting.' Mr Kinnaird the Stationmaster at Birnam also provides a good pen portrait. 'Mr Kinnaird is a rather fine looking old gentleman, with a long white beard tinged with yellow, a bluff red face, tall and sprucely dressed in a stationmaster's blue frock-coat with brass buttons. His defects of person are obvious when he walks, particularly so to us, having a bird's-eye view of the goods' yard which he constantly crosses at a rapid shuffle, coming from his house to the station. He turns his toes in, perhaps the least thing bandy, goes fast with a rolling gait and short steps, always with his hands in his pockets and looking towards his toes over an expanse of waist-coat and somewhat florid watch-chain.'

Throughout the *Journal* – and the letters, which I have hardly touched on here – we are constantly impressed by just how much Beatrix noticed as she went about the country. And she appears to have had the same compulsion to record in words as she had in drawings. While her paintings and sketches have long been appreciated, it seems to me that far too little attention has been paid to these wonderful verbal descriptions, in which, unlike her art work, her people are as good as her scenery. As we have already seen in the little books, it is often the incidentals rather than the descriptions which stick in the mind, together with that touch of wry humour which observes human failings with a certain detachment. In 1885 she tells us that from 10 December all dogs are to be muzzled – she merely records a fact – but then adds the comment, 'A most blessed change. Now, when I am set upon by three collies at once in the High Street, I simply smack them with my umbrella and laugh.' Every holiday provided passages which I should wish to quote had I time, but you must all read the letters and the *Journal* for yourselves, to appreciate to the full Beatrix Potter as an observer and recorder of the social scene. I will just end my talk with one of my favourite quotations, because it shows why her descriptions are so apt – she would have no truck with purple passages or with pretentiousness. Here she is, demolishing what is still a favourite English seaside resort, Torquay, known (to itself at any rate) as the English Riviera. She was there in 1893 and wrote, 'There are only three almond trees in Torquay, I have seen them all and they are small ones'. And that is that!

References

The quotations in this article are taken from the following sources:

The Journal of Beatrix Potter, 1881–1897, Complete edition. Transcribed from her code writings by Leslie Linder. New foreword by Judy Taylor. New rev. ed. F. Warne, 1989.

Letters to Children from Beatrix Potter. Collected and introduced by Judy Taylor. F. Warne, 1992.

The quotations from the 'Peter Rabbit' books are taken from the original and authorised editions.

Beatrix Potter: One of Nature's Conservatives

ROBERT LEESON

FOR THE MORE sensitive among the lovers of her books, Beatrix Potter the politician has an awesome aspect, emphatic, passionate, even violent in her opinions: reactionary (attached to past values), imperialist (in the Victorian sense of upholding Empire), and xenophobic (derogatory of Germans, Welsh, Irish, even despising foreign dogs). She turned her back on the Liberal politics of her beloved family, was hostile to Socialists, trade unions, state education, the urban working class, indeed all things urban – except perhaps for art galleries.

Yet her life's achievement, outside literature, was embodied in the public acquisition of land, often in the teeth of entrepreneurs, which today enables people of every class and nation to leave the shadow of the towns and bask in the sunlit countryside. One may also add that she hated 'official Tories' and, in her old age, took to her heart a pair of Pekinese.

Like every figure worth the study, she was full of hidden contradictions: hidden partly because she was often not aware of them herself, but mainly because only some five per cent of her writings were public (her election leaflets). Perhaps ten per cent were private – her letters (which we know mainly thanks to Judy Taylor and Jane Crowell Morse). The rest were secret – her journals (which we can now read thanks to Leslie Linder's decoding work).

Would she welcome our peering into her mind? I doubt it. But the investigation is worth taking that risk, since when we see her warts and all, Beatrix Potter, whom I would call 'one of nature's conservatives' shines all the brighter, not just as a writer, but as a fully paid-up member of the human community.

In the 1880s, when she began to write down her thoughts, the Potter family had not long moved to Kensington, from the grime of the industrial north-west of England. The Potters were upwardly mobile: Kensington had eight times as many servants per thousand of the population as any of the Lancashire towns they had known.

Though her journals contain derisive references to 'middle men pushing up', she was immensely proud of the Potter family, and of their marriage partners the Cromptons and Leeches. And they most definitely had worked their way up the social scale.

Her paternal grandfather, one time textile handworker, then millowner became a Whig-Liberal MP after the Reform Act of 1832 had opened Westminster to the manufacturing middle-classes.

Her family personified one side of the way English politics have divided since the Civil War of the 1640s when Parliament fought the King. The Whigs roughly represented the Parliamentary merchant-craftsmen, the improving landlord class and the Dissenters or Nonconformists in religion. Their opponents, the Tories, represented the King's party, the feudal landowners and their tenants, and the Established Church of England.

John Bradshaw, who signed Charles I's death warrant, married a Potter woman. In 1895, Beatrix Potter remarked that she was no undue admirer of the Royal Martyr. Another Potter was jailed for libelling a bishop. Abraham Crompton, Beatrix's forbear, bought Chorley Hall in Lancashire when it was confiscated from its Tory owner who had supported the Old Pretender in 1715.

These strange terms 'Tory' and 'Whig' are mutual abuse. Whig is a Scots term for cattle rustler, Tory an Irish word for raider. By the nineteenth century, new respectable names were sought. Tories became Conservatives, Whigs became Liberals. The change was slow. In November 1885 Beatrix wrote, 'though I am a Whig'. During the 1910 General Election, *The Kensington Post* published a letter from a Conservative voter complaining that the old insulting term 'Tory' still stuck to his party – as it does today.

The Potters were Unitarians. Unitarians were a small branch of Dissenting opinion but they were intellectual and charismatic. In the 1880s all mayors of major industrial towns were Unitarians. Yet Unitarians were excluded from the universities of Oxford and Cambridge in the mid-nineteenth century and Rupert Potter, Beatrix's father, had to get his higher education elsewhere.

He became a lawyer, but did not practise. He entered the rentier life in Kensington on inherited money, and like many other upwardly mobile men, shifted his allegiance to the Tories. Beatrix herself admired the Conservative leader Disraeli and detested the Liberal Gladstone.

In her late teens Beatrix was alone at home – her loved younger brother Bertram being sent away to private school. Over and above the instruction from governesses, she studied with enormous energy, art, history, literature, but above all politics. Though it is evident that she did not get on well with her mother, it is also evident that her father encouraged her explicitly and implicitly.

On the advancement of women Beatrix was ambivalent. She was contemptuous of the radical chic of 1884 who divided their time between 'fashion and women's rights'. But in January 1883 she wrote that a picture by artist Angelica Kauffman 'shows what a woman has done'. And, a few weeks before her death in 1943 she was satisfied that 'the right women are exercising an increased and hopeful influence in all spheres'.

Though she was encouraged to study, her life was restricted. At eighteen she longed to travel abroad, but she never left mainland Britain (though Judy Taylor points out to me that she once called briefly in Belfast). She was eighteen before she ever saw the Strand in London and thirty before she saw the inside of a City church. She knew London mainly from historical maps. As to the traditional interests of the teenage girl her diary has little to say. Of the party held on 18 June 1885, which perhaps served as a sort of coming out party, she remarked 'the first since ten years, and for my part may it suffice for ten more'.

Yet as both natural scientist and artist, she was a keen observer of both animal and human behaviour. And she developed a scepticism which tempered some of her political enthusiasms.

And enthusiasms they were. For Beatrix between the ages of sixteen and twenty, politics, next to art, were the breath of life. Her *Journal* pages teem with skilfully summarised editorials and reports, Parliamentary debates, accounts of political meetings – all second-hand. She attended one rally, a Tory election celebration in late 1885, but the crowd and noise made her wish to see the end of it.

Yet more fascinating are the snippets of gossip from her father's dining-table or club, and the chit-chat of Kensington drawing-rooms. She remarked wryly that when calling one always hopes the person will be out. But once there, she listened and recorded with the writer's ear. There was a great deal to record – both official and unofficial – because during the 1880s the political mould was being broken in a way far more decisive than during the Social Democratic episode of the 1980s.

For sixty years after the Reform Bill of 1832, the Liberals under Palmerston, and then Gladstone, dominated British political life. In November 1885, Beatrix wrote, 'In future days people will not be able to realise how completely England has been under the thumb of that shifting, incapable old man.' Seven years later, with Gladstone Prime Minister yet again Queen Victoria said much the same (the Queen's and Beatrix's views often coincided). If we can imagine a Junior Minister from a 1930s Government becoming Prime Minister in 1992, we get the picture.

Photograph of William Ewart
Gladstone by Rupert Potter,
dated 28 July 1884

The charismatic Tory leader, Disraeli, died in 1881. The anniversary of his death, Primrose Day, began to be a rallying point. On 23 April 1883, Beatrix noted: 'Primroses were worn by an extraordinary number of people when you consider that some fifty per cent are indifferent'. She added misleadingly: 'I should say the Conservatives aren't in a large minority'.

The chief challenge to the Whig-Liberal hierarchy came not from the Tories but from its own radical wing. The first divisive issue was equality, rich and poor, privilege and rights. Successive Acts of 1832, 1867 and 1884, swelled the number of male voters and the number of party activists. This upsurge from below was not universally welcome among families like the Potters of Kensington. Beatrix told the story of her grandmother's family. A humble suitor following a daughter home from chapel was ordered to be doused under the pump by the footman. 'So much for equality.'

From her grandmother Beatrix learned confusingly that the Luddites or machine-breakers of the 1800s thought that all men should be equal. In fact the Luddites were closer to her than she realised. They too found that technological change had come on too fast. Beatrix's diary often refers to arrivistes or 'jump ups', of the dangers of marriage across the social divide. One reference to a son of a wealthy family secretly marrying a miner's daughter is strangely prophetic of Bertram's later marriage. Bertram's disastrous entry to Charterhouse in 1886, which showed the perils of upward mobility, affected Beatrix deeply.

Even more than with 'jump ups', Beatrix was angry with middle-class people who by extravagant talk of equality, gave the wrong impression to the lower classes. She spoke of 'radical roughs' at election reform meetings, where the 'only persons of importance' could be counted on one hand.

She noted the earnings of needlewomen or cab drivers, but was careful not to conclude that they were too low. She was concerned about miners getting drunk on pay day. When an Irish guest discussed poverty, she wrote: 'It is refreshing, in these days of talk and sentimental nonsense about poverty, to hear him talk of it as a stubborn commonplace fact.' But would the newly emancipated masses accept it as such? She felt that the new working class voters were 'rather conservative [small c] on the whole, very loyal, and tenacious of England's honour.' The danger came from mischievous radicals who stirred up trouble – like Joseph Chamberlain.

On the Tory side there were also radicals, such as Randolph Churchill (father of Winston) who, said Beatrix, 'are viewed with mingled hope and fear'. If she had known that Churchill was privately meeting H.M. Hyndman, leader of the small Socialist grouping, to discuss social reform, she would have been more suspicious of him. In those days, with the Labour Party some two decades in the future, people campaigning for social solutions lobbied both main parties. Hyndman told Churchill, 'the leading Conservatives would oppose such proposals as a matter of business if fathered by the Liberals. The Liberals could not afford to resist them if proposed by the Conservatives for fear of losing popularity.'

Such was the charisma of Chamberlain and Churchill, that people were talking of a third and fourth party emerging. Yet for all the turbulence of the 1880s, Gladstone kept on top like a man made of cork, by consummate skill or by deviousness, according to your view. This made him a legend, the butt of innumerable lampoons and rumours spread by exasperated opponents. Beatrix's *Journal* is an archive for such stories. It contains, I think, seventy-four references to Gladstone, seventy of them derisive, ironic, or abusive.

'Papa says it is Gladstone's fault', 'Gladstone is reported to have a cold', but '[Gladstone] is nót ill – the Baxters said not', Gladstone is 'out of his mind', Gladstone's dress is compared to that of a 'nigger minstrel'. He is a 'shuffler'. 'This will cost him his conscience.' He is an 'old fox'. The 'old lunatic will soon stand alone'. She repeated what she called 'wicked stories' believing them to be 'perfectly true'. Lady Eastlake told her in confidence that Mrs Gladstone was a 'terrible slut'. Her father (in the middle of the 1886 riots) whispered of something about Gladstone that 'he cannot mention to ladies'. When Tennyson died she wished it were Gladstone, and in early 1885 she declared 'Oh if some lunatic had shot old Gladstone twelve months since'.

" TOO LATE ! "

Telegram, Thursday Morning, Feb, 5.—" Khartoum taken by the Mahdi. General Gordon's fate uncertain."

John Tenniel's *Punch* cartoon of 14th February 1885. The caption reads:
'Khartoum taken by the Mahdi. General Gordon's fate uncertain'.

This last outburst was caused by 'Awful news just sent from Egypt, Khartoum fallen, Gordon a prisoner, Sir Charles Wilson and part of the army blocked up under heavy fire'. The fate of General Gordon, killed by Sudanese Islamic rebels, stirred up a tremendous outcry, fanned by an increasingly Empire-minded Press. Queen Victoria told Gladstone that he had murdered Gordon. So high was feeling that the normally correct Rupert Potter, who was on speaking terms with Gladstone, yet brushed past him in the street without raising his hat. 'I'd ... have given him my mind,' tartly observed Beatrix.

28

Orthodox Liberals believed individuals and nations should determine their own destiny. But this was at odds with the steady growth in England's colonial possessions to which nearly two million people were emigrating every decade. In the 1840s the writer Captain Marryat foresaw when England 'would no longer boast of her possessions throughout the world.' But in 1898 the equally liberal novelist Rider Haggard said he did not believe in the Divine Right of Kings but did believe in the 'Divine Right of a Civilising People' to rule the world.

Non-intervention and self-determination in fact clashed with the other classic Liberal doctrine, Free Trade. As British goods sought markets around the world, merchants abroad demanded protection from hostile local régimes and this led to a series of annexations from Burma to Transvaal to Egypt, and thus to colonial wars, seventy-five of them in Victoria's reign. As Kipling sang: 'Walk wide of the Widow of Windsor, for half of creation she owns.'

The opening of the Suez Canal inexorably led to British troops invading Egypt to quell Arabi Pasha's revolt. Beatrix, excited, regretted the bloodshed and reported the family friend, the radical John Bright, calling for Arabi Pasha to be treated with honour. She went with her father to join crowds welcoming the troops home. Later in 1884 she noted with regret how little fuss was made when the second contingent arrived home.

When the Mahdi led the Sudanese in revolt against Egyptian rule, retired British officers led Egyptian troops as mercenaries against them. Beseiged in Khartoum, the call went up for them to be rescued. Beatrix and most of the public believed that the British troops were trapped. The Press did not enlighten them. Gordon's ill-starred one-man bid to organise evacuation (his idea) led to disaster, and the blame fell on the hesitating Liberal Government. Rightly or wrongly, Gordon's death triggered a period of strong Empire bias in British foreign and commercial policy. Beatrix reflected the shift in opinion, exulting in 'great spirit' in the colonies for a war with Russia over Constantinople, and cheered by the launching of 'new ironclads'. (This is the time of the Music Hall song 'We don't want to fight; but, by Jingo, if we do, We've got the ships, we've got the men, we've got the money too.') Beatrix also ridiculed an attempt by a Radical MP to move a vote of censure over the annexation of Burma.

What complicated matters for Gladstone was that while Radicals like Bright were for non-intervention, Radicals like Dilke or Chamberlain were strongly imperialist. They saw in Empire the solution to the problems of poverty at home. Unemployment grew day by day. Beatrix reported one thousand building workers rushing to sign on for work on the new Peking Railway. She felt sorry for the workless, but was hostile to agitators or reformers. German and American competition pressed hard on the British economy. The fact was that Free Trade built the Empire, but in the end the two were incompatible. There was talk of making the Empire a 'self-sufficing world'. Yet official policy was still Free Trade, the motor of capitalist expansion.

In June 1885 Beatrix noted that the Government was fending off an attack over Gordon, but was defeated over legislation on beer. 'There is one thing to be said about this defeat, it is against this absurd so-called Free Trade principle which taxes British instead of foreign produce.'

Of course protectionists like Beatrix were usually not entirely consistent. She thought that the annexation of Burma was 'one of the most fortunate foreign events in British trade .... Burma itself is a large country but if the Chinese trade could be opened up, it would be the saving of cotton and iron.'

On home and foreign affairs, therefore, the young diarist of Bolton Gardens was speaking for a large section of Liberal support, making Gladstone's tightrope-walking increasingly impossible. The issue which brought him down was Ireland. The Act of Union of 1801 bound the smaller country to the larger, with Irish MPs in the House of Commons. But national sentiment aggravated by the sufferings of the Famine led to Irish agitation against English absentee landlords. Charles Stuart Parnell united the Irish, both Catholic and Protestant in a single demand: Home Rule. Classic Liberal sentiment compelled support. But the *status quo* demanded law and order in Ireland with dire results. Parnell's movement was peaceful but had its violent fringe. In March 1883, Beatrix wrote: 'What will be blown up next?' Of course Gladstone was to blame. 'He takes the side of these rogues and then, if they think he is slackening, they frighten him on a bit – really we shall be as bad as France soon.' Here her view accurately reflected *The Times* editorials. The *Journal* is full of fascinating detail. Her father saw the Chief of Police shadowing Parnell on the Brighton train. A neighbour, Lady Florence Dixie, claimed to have been mugged by Fenians. Beatrix was sceptical. But she regarded the claim that the police planted a detonator on an Irishman as 'monstrous'. Gladstone, she said, was offering terms to Home Rulers 'at any price'.

People opposed to Home Rule in both England and Ulster took their stand by the Act of Union. The 'Unionists' became the real third force in politics. Men like Chamberlain and even old Radical John Bright were against Home Rule. In the House of Commons, Parnell's group, to put pressure on Gladstone, tactically supported the Tories. At the 1885 General Election, they urged Irish people in Britain to vote Tory. This made even the partisan nineteen-year-old Beatrix uneasy: 'I wish the Conservatives would get a large enough majority to work without Home Rulers.' However, the General

Election, on which she reports with gusto, delivered deadlock, with eighty-six Irish MPs holding the balance and Gladstone still in office.

Gladstone began to put together a package radical enough to please one side, limited enough to mollify the other. Reading the plan leaked to *The Standard* newspaper, Beatrix, not for the first time, declared him to be mad. But it was clear that the Liberal Party could not stand another year's tug-of-war over Home Rule. In April 1886 Beatrix reported: 'They are inclined to stick to Gladstone, but Chamberlain's attitude has unsettled all their plans.' That month Chamberlain resigned his government post, led ninety-three unionist Liberals into the lobby against Home Rule and effectively brought the Government down. At the following General Election, seventy-eight Liberal Unionists were returned and they remained as a separate group until they merged with the Tories in 1909.

Beneath this political turmoil, there was a deeper undercurrent of unrest over poverty and unemployment. H.M. Hyndman, the Socialist leader, claimed that twenty-five per cent of Londoners lived in dire poverty. Charles Booth the philanthropist considered this was 'grossly overstated' and launched a massive social inquiry to get at the truth. Years later, the inquiry established the figure as thirty-one per cent. Poverty was real and the patience of the unemployed running out.

On 8 February 1886, Beatrix wrote: 'The Riot: To think that I should live to see such a day. It is most terrible and alarming . . . . We narrowly missed being in it. I went with Mother to the stores . . . in the Haymarket . . . . A good many rough men and workmen going along Piccadilly . . . . They kept dodging across under the horse's head.'

From *The Times* next day she learnt that Hyndman had addressed a rally of nearly 30,000 people in Trafalgar Square. She added, 'I will record nothing but that which came to us from observation.' Reynolds (their coachman) was a store of information, about carriages attacked and stones used from street repairs. 'They did not attack the Reform [Club] . . . . The servants . . . and many members of the Club were on the steps watching and laughing.' That evening Papa added a vivid picture of rioters fighting police in Pall Mall. By 10 February there were wild rumours of troop movements. 'Someone in authority will be a scapegoat . . . . No one seems to lay the blame on the working men, it is the Jacobins, roughs and thieves.'

'There is some talk of the lady who was attacked in Piccadilly and escaped, bidding her coachman "drive over the dogs". I trust she said nothing so vulgar, but she had strong provocation . . . . Thick fog. Met Dr Sadler, who said they were in a great state at Hampstead . . . . Numbers of rough looking men about the streets here in South Kensington . . . . Discussion as to locking front gate. The Government show no sign of moving . . . . Old Gladstone only comes to town today . . . . It is scandalous.' 11 February. 'Rumours of a mob of ten thousand roughs from Greenwich . . . who however did not arrive . . . . Bridges were guarded, the troops held in readiness at the barracks and a guard at the banks'. More 'rough looking men . . . whatever may be their means, most of them are fat and well fed, a good many smoking, some in gloves, mostly addicted to bright coloured neckties . . . . [They] looked first at the Brougham, and then at Reynolds and the mare, such a scowl. I should have been terrified had they formed part of a crowd.'

'A great many people are leaving town . . . . Father has given £30 to the Lord Mayor's Fund.' (Hyndman later noted sardonically that the Fund rose from £2,000 to £75,000 in a matter of days.) 'It seems generally believed the government will collapse within a month . . . . Father says he will be sorry if the Tories have to deal with this business.'

12 February: 'People . . . will believe the faintest rumour . . . . My mother is continually listening for sounds outside . . . . My father is becoming very yellow and lower than ever . . . . Talks about going to the Colonies, Edinburgh, quiet provincial towns, but he has done that occasionally for the last ten years . . . . Reynolds [their coachman] . . . has a policeman friend who tells him grisly things in the late evening, which when duly reported after breakfast and together with *The Times*, give my father a turn for the day.'

On 17 February 1886 Hyndman and his fellow Socialists Burns and Champion went on trial at Bow Street. 'They are being treated with every consideration, Counsel, adjournment, it is scandalous. Why, they ought to be hung at once like dogs.'

The arrival in London of the Abbé Liszt with his ability to stretch eleven notes with ease distracted her a moment, then Beatrix was busy with Parliamentary debates again. 'If the Commons will pass this [the Home Rule Bill] they will pass anything. The repudiation of the National Debt, or the Commune with Hyndman as 1st. magistrate.'

Worse was to follow. On 10 April the Socialists were acquitted, the judge having ruled there was no case to answer. 'The whole thing was a farce, Russell who prosecuted, is himself a Socialist as well as a Home Ruler.'

Russell, however, was Sir Charles Russell, and in the words of *The Times* historian 'the foremost advocate of his day'. His junior, Asquith, later became Prime Minister. He did his best to convict Hyndman but failed. He did better a year or two later in the inquiry into the Parnell letters. *The Times* had bought these believing they proved Parnell was hand in glove with the dynamiters. Russell easily proved they were forgeries. The cost of the inquiry plunged *The Times* into bankruptcy.

But none of this drama appeared in Beatrix's diary for she had become ill. At the end of 1886 she wrote: 'I made a last feeble attempt at notes in July last, being excited much by the General Election, but since then there were not half a dozen words on paper.'

She never recovered her fine frenzy for party politics. The political references of the 1890s are fewer, more detached. Losing even her anti-Gladstone zest she saw him at the private view for the Millais portrait and said 'however one may dislike him, he has a face one would notice unknown in a crowd'. On the same day, she told her imaginary friend Esther: 'keep this silly letter – it will be amusing fifty years hence, when the Irish question is settled and the ladies wear panniers and peaked waists.'

Beatrix's political passion lasted for about four years. Was it just a girl's enthusiasm picked up from family, older friends and reading? That would be to underestimate her. At the age of seventeen she may write 'Papa says ...', but at eighteen she remarked: 'The traditions of our family kept him from speaking out. I sometimes think if he had a little more courage to take the other side, he would be less worried.' And later, 'I don't think grandmamma's opinion of his politics could be made worse than it is already.' She (Beatrix) 'would vote Tory'. With increasing frequency she expressed independent points of view.

By the early 1900s, because of her writing, financial independence was coming her way and she was ready to break out of the constraints of a sheltered life. And break out she did. At the 1910 General Election she took to the streets. Foreign competition and growing unemployment gave mass appeal to the demand for Tariff Reform against Liberal Free Trade. Beatrix wrote to a friend in January 1910: 'I am so busy over the Election, my fingers are quite stiff with drawing posters'. It was a personal matter. Her merchandising of Peter Rabbit had been frustrated by pirated dolls imported from Germany. The South London Toy Trade, said her posters, had been killed by free trade with Germany. She wrote a leaflet on Tariff Reform and when her publishers Warne could not produce it for her, went round the print shops herself. Printers, she thought, were rather odd people. 'I once met with one specimen from Hatton Garden, who said he was a sample of his work fellows; "socialist" was a mild word for him.'

Later in January, pleased with the result of the elections in Kensington and Windermere (though the Liberal Government held on to power), she told Harold Warne: 'I promise faithfully to return to pigs and mice, next week.' But within weeks another General Election loomed and she was back on the trail, this time with an illustrated leaflet aimed at farmers, protesting over plans to register horses for requisition in a future war. 'It is useless to talk to farmers about dolls,' she told Wilfred Evans, her new-found printer. 'But if there *is* a subject which enrages us – it is meddling with our horses.' She added wryly: 'I should sign it "N.Lancs" as a female farmer is silly on paper, though well informed.' In April though, she was 'enjoying a spicy correspondence with a Socialist in *The Western Morning News*', who was 'under the delusion that I am a gentleman.' Male attitudes notwithstanding, we find her round the bus depots in London, where the drivers took the horse leaflet 'with avidity'.

Meanwhile she revised her leaflet linking the protection of copyright overseas with restrictions on foreign imports. She was glad to see that trade unions had taken up the copyright question, remarking tartly that she 'cannot understand their attitude to tariff reform, when they are such extreme protectionists themselves in the matter of labour.'

Beatrix Potter's design for a poster in favour of Tariff Reform, made for the 1910 General Election

She saw Tariff Reform as needed since 'the book trade is powerless in itself', and 'I am afraid the book trade by itself will never make anything of the United States.'

Her campaign lasted several months. It was vigorous, eccentric and, for her, thoroughly enjoyable. And it was totally her own. In January she declined Harold Warne's invitation to write to *The Times*, or to enlist Peter Rabbit in the efforts then being made to get a Copyright Protection Bill through Parliament. This would, she thought 'drag the little book into Radical politics'. This presumably refers to the fact that the Liberal Government was sympathetic to Copyright Reform – if not Trade Protection.

On the other hand, having difficulties with the printing of her leaflets in certain quarters, she declared in a letter to Evans the printer on 8 March: 'I cannot stand official Tories'. Invited to address what is obviously a Tory election meeting in Kendal (20 January) she had 'no difficulty in resisting that temptation'.

She was pro-Unionist and pro-Tory in sentiment and remained so but never (as far as my researches can discover) did she join the Tory Party either in Kensington or the Lake District. Nor did she, save once in a 1933 letter to Joe Moscrop, the shepherd, ever refer to Free Trade again.

Her letters to Louie Choyce, her work companion, to her cousin Caroline and to various American friends, contain many clues to her political thinking. In 1924 she was famously indignant over a newspaper story confusing her with Beatrice Webb, the Socialist (maiden name Potter, but no relation if you please). In 1932 she showed a shrewd awareness of the vulnerability of the National Government at by-elections.

Throughout the 1930s she brooded on the rise of Hitler 'the fear of war ... the shame of being bullied', but was sceptical of the League of Nations' policy to deter aggression. At the time of the 1938 Munich crisis, she felt 'Chamberlain could do no other than give in'. Though by December of that year she declared, exasperated, that there was 'no limit to what Chamberlain will agree to'.

That is not her only change of heart. In March 1936, she welcomed the new King Edward VIII: 'How clearly and firmly he spoke'. But by December she told an American friend: 'I sometimes wonder whether England is not under an obligation to Mrs Simpson.' For her the abdication was 'good riddance to bad rubbish'. Her switches of opinion were not untypical for English people of the time, Tory or not. One must look deeper than mere opinions to find the real roots of Beatrix Potter's politics. Hers was a small 'c' conservatism made up of different elements.

First was a heartfelt preference for country over town. 'I do wish we lived in the country' she wrote in late 1884. Ten years later, she juxtaposed the 'rag bag riot of the towns' with 'good Mother Earth'. In the desperate summer of 1940 she wrote: 'And the mountains and fells and green land of pleasant England will survive her smoky towns and ugly suburbs'.

Two years later, she recalled: 'my brother and I hated London'. Distaste for towns spilled over on to their population. In 1916 she grumbled at high pay for munition workers. Wages, she asserted in 1926, 'are enormous'. 'People [1930] want something for nothing'. In 1933 she spoke of the 'menace' of trade unions. And in the Second World War, she found, again, that 'factory workers are paid more than is good for them,' though two years later, she spoke complacently of the subsidy which had trebled wool prices for farmers. Her comic assertion in January 1942 that war workers complained of the size of the tea ration because they were drinking 'immoderate quantities' matched oddly with her child-like pleasure in the food parcels from the United States.

But perhaps hostility to town workers reached its most embarrassing expression in 1938 with the fear of being 'swarmed over with refugees from Barrow. No one would grudge asylum in a raid, but the dockers' families are rough, mostly Irish Catholics'. Still, her snobbery, such as it was, could not resist her awareness later on of the 'cruel destruction' of towns in the Blitz, nor her admiration for the 'wonderful spirit' of townsfolk under bombing. In any case she was never mean with her beloved countryside. Townsfolk on holiday were welcome to enjoy themselves, she wrote in 1913, provided that they shut the gates. And in 1928 she described in warm terms the sight of holiday-makers sitting on the grass in an area by Lake Windermere whose purchase she had organised.

Along with the town-country contradiction went an even deeper feeling – an attachment to the past, the recording of old people's memories, the cherishing of old buildings and furniture, and apprehension about time to come. In May 1884, nearly eighteen, she wrote: 'The future is dark and uncertain, let me keep the past.' Change alarmed her: 'I don't know what will come to this country soon, it is going at a tremendous speed.' And two years later: 'Changes are to be treated with the greatest caution and only granted when really desired or needed.'

In 1924 she was sure that 'nice old fashioned people' who read her books, would be upset at the confusion between herself and Socialist Beatrice Webb. In 1920 she was sarcastic about 'the samples of modern child that emerge from the hotels'. By contrast in 1928, she saw her work as helping 'small children on the road to honest simple pleasures' such as those offered by the Scouts and Guides.

Another five years on and she found that 'education has got out of hand'. In 1936 she was scathing about the 'average English child'. In that year, she wrote to Joe Moscrop, comprehensively: 'there is much that us old ones don't like in modern life.' In the summer of 1940 she recalled the early 1900s when Lakeland 'was unsullied by Morris cars "en masse". What a world; mechanized to destruction.'

Beatrix's nostalgia and resistance to change were not simply negative qualities, perhaps first and foremost because of Canon H.D. Rawnsley whom she met at the age of sixteen and with whom she remained friends for many years. One has only to read his book *Life and Nature at the English Lakes* with its celebration of tradition, custom and dialect, of countryside enjoyed by happy, well-behaved crowds, and his horror of trippers 'leaving the ground

Beatrix Potter with Canon Hardwicke Rawnsley and his
son, photographed by Rupert Potter at Lingholm in the
Lake District

horribly bottle bestrewn' to recognise his influence. Yet Beatrix Potter still
had her own agenda. Step by step she worked out her plan with almost
instinctive determination, to get back to her northern roots, back down the
time tunnel to a world where life, closer to nature, would move more slowly,
and its values would be preserved from destructive change.

For her, conservatism meant above all conservation. In 1911, soon after
the famous election campaign, she was in action against the 'beastly aero-
planes' which disturbed the peace of Lake Windermere. The agitation defeated the menace, though she observed tartly that she got more support from
the radicals than from the aristocrats.

In 1920 she discussed the letting of land for a bowling green, emphasising
the need to consider the interests of the public at large, not just those of one
interest group. 1922 found her buying up house contents before the dealers

could get at them. Her letters in the 1920s show a shrewd appreciation of the difference between planning regulations for cities and for small country towns, and a rational view of what should be preserved and what let go. Writing about Troutbeck Park, acquired by her efforts for the National Trust, she laid down as a matter of principle that 'a good, intelligent solvent tenant, is preferable to a rack rent.' Three years later on and she made critical comments about 'Windermere society that yachts, golfs and plays tennis with a strong leaven of Manchester and Liverpool', while she saw things from the angle of the 'village smithy and the joiner's shop'.

Beatrix Potter was a landowner and she owned more and more land as time passed, but she saw herself as a working landowner. Like Bertram, her brother, as she noted in 1918, she believed very much in the value of 'useful manual work'. 'Careless landlords,' she argued in 1931, make 'careless tenants' while 'an absentee landlord with a typical land agent', she thought in 1929, were responsible for 'what Socialism exists in the countryside'.

How was a conservative who loved the Cumbrian land and rural way of life to hold off the encroaching tide of the commercial developer? In 1934 she still trusted that private ownership and public opinion might be enough. But two years later she wrote to Mrs Rawnsley (October 1934): 'The Canon's original aim for complete preservation of as much property as possible by acquisition, was the right one for the Lake District.'

Thus Beatrix fulfilled her life-long dreams by a sustained individual process of taking land into public ownership. Her small 'c' conservatism found lasting expression in a small 's' socialist form. Throughout the sixty odd years that Beatrix Potter was a political animal her views ranged far and wide, often switching and changing. But her fundamental ideas were constant. At the age of seventy-six, tired and ill, she could still say resolutely 'after the war there will be some tidying up to do'. And only weeks before her death, she could say with quiet satisfaction: 'I have survived . . .'. And, thanks to her special brand of conservatism, so has a considerable part of the Lake District.

If you would see her memorial, look around you.

References

Beatrix Potter quotations before 1900 are from:
The Journal of Beatrix Potter, 1881–1897, Complete edition. Transcribed from her code writings by Leslie Linder, New foreword by Judy Taylor. New rev. ed. F. Warne, 1989

After 1900, quotations are from her letters in:
Beatrix Potter's Letters: A selection by Judy Taylor, F. Warne, 1989
Beatrix Potter's Americans. Edited by Jane Crowell Morse, Horn Book, Boston, Mass. 1982
Additional (unpublished) letters from 1910, quoted on page *33*, courtesy Judy Taylor

Beatrix Potter and the London Art Scene in the 1880s and 1890s

MICHAEL WILSON

ON 13 JANUARY 1883 the 17-year-old Beatrix Potter wrote in her *Journal* as follows: 'Been to the Winter Exhibition of Old Masters at the Academy. I had been looking forward to it very much, but I never thought it would be like this. I never thought there *could* be such pictures. It is almost too much to see them all at once – just fancy seeing five magnificent Van Dycks side by side, before *me* who never thought to see one. It is rather a painful pleasure, but I have seldom felt such a great one.'

In these days when art is so universally available, her genuine enthusiasm comes as a shock. We take for granted the accessibility of museums and art galleries, of books, television, and all the other modern visual aids that were mostly denied to Beatrix. In addition, her own situation was made even more difficult by the cloistered manner of her upbringing and education. In the 1880s, however, things began to change somewhat for her, and it was deemed that she was now of an age at which it was safe to introduce her to the wider art world outside the confines of her schoolroom and beyond the tuition of governesses and drawing teachers. At the same time, her *Journal* shows that she was already a good deal more worldly-wise than her parents probably realised.

In the 1880s and '90s the London art scene revolved around three principal centres of interest. These were: firstly, the Summer and Winter Exhibitions of the Royal Academy, the Summer Exhibition being then as now dedicated to new art, while the Winter Exhibition was reserved for Old Masters; secondly, important commercial galleries, amongst which the Grosvenor Gallery took pride of place (the Grosvenor also held Winter Exhibitions of Old Masters); thirdly, the permanent collection at the National Gallery. All these figured in Beatrix Potter's life as she describes it in her *Journal*, and in addition she had personal experience of meeting various artists, especially Millais, who as you all know was a friend of the family and

A Private View Day at the Royal Academy, painted by William Powell Frith in 1881

greatly valued Rupert Potter's expertise in photography as an aid to his own work.

As one might expect, Beatrix was no more overawed by artists, whether singly or collectively, than she was by statesmen or herdsmen. Even the revered Millais was not immune from criticism. In 1884 she calls him 'a very uncertain man' (*Journal*, 5 May 1884), and in 1890 she dismisses one of his portraits of Gladstone as 'a shocking daub [which] does not do him justice at

all' (*Journal*, 4 February 1890). Sometimes, on looking back through her *Journal*, she came to revise sentiments or opinions which she had earlier expressed with all the intensity of youth. Her detailed account of her 1883 visit to the exhibition of Old Masters at the Royal Academy was supplemented a mere three years later by the following dismissive comment: 'Amazingly crude euphuistic criticism'. For the most part, however, her typically shrewd and hard-headed judgements on artists and their work are still valid, and still have the power to surprise us today, perhaps even to shock us, as will be seen. The principal showcase for contemporary art was the Summer Exhibition at the Royal Academy, initiated each year, then as now, by a private view which was more of a social than an artistic occasion. William Powell Frith painted the scene in 1881, one year before Beatrix made her first visit to the Academy. But while it is possible to identify some of the individuals in Frith's painting (such as Leighton, Gladstone, Oscar Wilde and Lily Langtry), Beatrix had a different attitude to the event. Of the private view in 1895 she wrote: 'As to the pictures, we saw them splendidly, but for the company, unfortunately neither my aunt nor I knew who people were, except Mr. and Mrs. Gladstone whom we met continually round corners . . .. However, there were many pretty dresses and a few sweet faces, and I daresay some (at least) of the haggard gentlemen were Dukes, and the smart ones, lights of literature, and I judged them all up to my own satisfaction.'

On occasions other than the private view, her Academy visits yielded better results on a personality basis, in particular a memorable description of Ruskin whom she spotted on 5 March 1884: 'Mr. Ruskin was one of the most ridiculous figures I have seen. A very old hat, much necktie and aged coat buttoned up on his neck, humpbacked, not particularly clean-looking. He had on high boots, and one of his trousers was tucked up on the top of one. He became aware of this half way round the room and stood on one leg to put it right, but in so doing hitched up the other trouser worse than the first one had been. He was making remarks on the pictures which were listened to with great attention by his party, an old lady and gentleman and a young girl, but other people evidently did not know him.' After such devastating comments it is difficult to take the Sage and his works seriously ever again. Not that the Potters did. 'Mr. Ruskin has got a study of laurel leaves at one of the water colour exhibitions. Papa says it is simply dreadful.' Nevertheless it has to be said that despite Rupert Potter's scorn Ruskin's sketches and finished watercolours are highly esteemed today.

The *Journal* records that Beatrix attended the Summer Exhibitions at the Royal Academy in 1882, '83, '84, '85 and '95, but she makes extended comments only for 1882 and 1885. She probably also went to them in the years between 1886 and 1894, but does not say so. The catalogues of the late-nineteenth century Summer Exhibitions are crammed with the names of painters who, while faithfully and competently reflecting the tastes and enthusiasms of their own day, are now almost completely forgotten. But while inevitably confronted by acres of unremarkable pictures, Beatrix also saw the work of artists who, though no longer so highly esteemed as in their own day, have nevertheless managed to remain on the fringes of acceptable nineteenth-century art. As examples of these we might take Benjamin

Leader, Marcus Stone and William Frederick Yeames. At the 1882 Exhibition, Leader produced *In the Evening There Shall be Light*, which Beatrix
describes as an 'immense landscape ... rather hard in parts but pleasing on
the whole', a judgement which could be safely applied to many of Leader's
dark-toned but visionary landscapes. Marcus Stone painted the kind of
costume drama which never convinces for a moment, but which is still
popular on greetings cards or as restaurant decoration. Number 5 in the 1882
catalogue, his *Il y a Toujours un Autre* is dismissed by Beatrix as 'flat,
sentimental, and unpleasant colour'. (It is now in the Tate Gallery and is
sometimes known as *A Prior Attachment*.) She expanded a little on this when
faced with number 222, entitled *Bad News*. 'Mr. Stone's pictures are spoilt by
being always the same kind of face [hear, hear!] and such a cold, low tone [i.e.
colour].' Bad News for Stone! Yeames is today best known for his *And When
Did You Last See Your Father?*, which is now in the Walker Art Gallery,
Liverpool. Beatrix saw his *Prince Arthur and Hubert*, but made no comment

Prince Arthur and Hubert
by William Frederick Yeames

43

on it; this is a pity, because it was bought at the 1882 Exhibition by Manchester City Art Gallery (where it still is), and it would have been interesting to know what she thought of it.

As an example of an inflated reputation now lost, we might take Briton Rivière, an artist highly esteemed in his time but now almost totally ignored. At the 1882 Academy Exhibition he showed, amongst others, a portrait of Beatrix's beautiful cousin Kate Potter with her poodle Figaro, entitled *Cupboard Love*. According to Beatrix 'he took a great deal of trouble over Kate and is very well satisfied with it, but it is certainly not good'. She further commented that she herself would not have recognised Kate, and that most of the picture was taken up by the cupboard. Years later she was to produce a tongue-in-cheek parody of the portrait in her picture of Duchess searching for the mouse pie in *The Tale of The Pie and the Patty-Pan*. Her uncle Edmund Crompton Potter had no less than eleven Rivières in his collection when it came up for sale in 1884 (including the portrait of Kate), but Beatrix was not deceived by quantity. It was quality she was after. 'Splendid pictures some of them, but I confess to being slightly disappointed with them .... Doubtless Rivière owes much of his success to the appeal which his pictures make to the feelings: the composition is tolerable, and the colour, but would hardly strike one in an ordinary picture .... Rivière certainly does not draw figures well.' Alas! figure drawing was also to prove one of her own weaknesses.

Another regular exhibitor whose reputation, in contrast, has remained relatively high, was Frederick Leighton. Although she makes little comment on his Academy pictures except to praise their colouring, Beatrix is generous in her praise of *The Mermaid*, one of two Leightons also owned by Edmund Potter. 'I have never been a great admirer of Leighton, certainly was not prejudiced in his favour. This work took me completely by surprise. I had no idea he could paint like that. A rich pure colour, powerful drawing, strong sentiment and beautiful composition, such as one has rarely seen equalled by a small "genre" picture, wholly untouched by the sickly unhealthy look which mars so many of Leighton's paintings. The colour of the sea was slightly crude, perhaps, but otherwise this picture was perfect in its way.' Leighton's blatant eroticism seems not to have touched her.

For Beatrix, Leighton, Millais and one or two others were constant beacons of quality in those years in which she felt that the Academy's Summer Exhibitions had little to offer. In 1885 for example, she wrote 'Been to the Academy, a most confusing number of pictures, whereof many might with advantage be sifted out. It seems to me that ... there are fewer bad pictures this year, but a very large number are uninteresting. There is such a want of originality or interesting detail'.

As for the works of painters from earlier ages, Beatrix got to know them

The Mermaid by Lord Leighton

mainly through the Winter Exhibitions of Old Masters which were held both at the Royal Academy and at the Grosvenor Gallery in New Bond Street. The Grosvenor was a private gallery opened in 1877 by the owner, Sir Coutts Lindsay, with a view to promoting the work of younger contemporary artists who, it was felt, were being unjustly ignored by the Academy. Here, as at the Academy itself, the Winter Exhibitions were something of a fill-up, though none the less valuable for that. At these two locations Beatrix was able to study great artists from the past in a way that she had never been able to do before. The 1883 Exhibition at the Academy provided her first taste of this experience – so how did it affect her, *vis-à-vis* the various artists?

Michelangelo and Fra Bartolommeo were a disappointment. Indeed Michelangelo was always to be a problem to Beatrix; a year later she saw at the National Gallery what was probably his *Entombment*, unfinished but still monumental, and wrote as follows: 'No one will read this. I say fearlessly that the Michelangelo is hideous and badly drawn; I wouldn't give tuppence for it except as a curiosity'. In contrast she found Titian's portrait of *Caterina Cornaro* to be 'the finest portrait of the Exhibition, if not the most beautiful picture'. (The portrait is now in the Washington National Gallery; it is no longer thought to be of Caterina Cornaro, and may not even be by Titian.) On the other hand, two portraits by Rembrandt she found 'powerful in their way, but if I had not known who they were by, I should not have looked at them with much interest.' (One knows the feeling.) It was here too that, on her own admission, she saw the work of the Dutch landscape artists for the first time. 'I was surprised and pleased, it seemed very honest sort of work, no use being made of anything impressive or extremes of light and shadow like in Turner's pictures. Every thing was calm and smooth like the scenery of Holland herself.' Rubens to her was 'bright, crude ... rich and animated'.

About Van Dyck she had mixed feelings, finding his portrait of the young Prince Charles (Charles II) another disappointment, but elsewhere was impressed by his bold naturalism and brilliant colours. In fact, she found that, of all the pictures at this 1883 Winter exhibition, she had been most impressed by the Van Dycks, by Titian's *Caterina Cornaro*, and by some of the paintings of Reynolds (of whom more very shortly). The exhibition, she wrote, 'has raised my idea of art, and I have learnt some things by it. I was rather disheartened at first, but I have got over it'. She went to this same Exhibition on two further occasions and found no reason to change her basic opinions, except that she was 'better pleased with Rembrandt'. Those two giants of late eighteenth-century English painting, Reynolds and Gainsborough, were still, in the late years of the nineteenth century, given what might seem today almost disproportionate attention, despite their undoubted stature. No less than twenty-two paintings by Reynolds figured in the 1883 Academy Winter Exhibition, and the 1884 Winter Exhibition at the Grosvenor Gallery was entirely devoted to his work. Although Beatrix has quite a lot to say about Reynolds, it must be admitted that on the whole her comments on him are not nearly as arresting as are those on other artists. Like many another gallery visitor both before and since her day, she seems to have been overwhelmed by the sheer quantity of Reynolds's work, as well as by its highly variable quality. She was also on occasion frustrated by the devastating combination of yellowed varnish and Reynolds's often unfortunate choice of pigments, many of which were badly faded even by the 1880s. As samples of the pictures she saw at, for example, the Grosvenor 1884 Winter Exhibition, we may take three, the first being Reynolds's self-portrait as President of the Royal Academy, which to Beatrix 'seemed a very fine picture but not like most. It struck me at the first glance as like a chalk drawing in black and red'. She was unaware that in it Reynolds was consciously parodying Rembrandt's painting *Aristotle with the Bust of Homer*. The second is a famous portrait described by Beatrix with unconscious humour as 'the splendid and majestic *Mrs. Siddons* in tolerable condition'. The third is *The Three Ladies Waldegrave*, of which Beatrix remarks 'it was rather faded but perhaps these wonderful harmonies of pearly grey are more beautiful than brighter colours. I liked the lady on the left best, she had so much expression'.

Mrs Siddons as the Tragic Muse
by Sir Joshua Reynolds

Beatrix summed up her impressions of the contrasting portrait techniques of Reynolds and Gainsborough as follows: 'Reynolds presents to us a cheerful, pleasant race, the men refined, kindly and thoughtful, the women fresh, gay, natural and clothed in rich colour. Gainsborough's men are solid and commonplace, careworn instead of cheerful, the ladies long-faced and depressed ... and dressed in hoops, tight stays and cardboard waistcoats'. She could have added, but did not, that Reynolds painted his sitters as they wished to be seen, while Gainsborough painted people as he saw them. Beatrix was fascinated by *The Blue Boy* and considered it to be one of Gainsborough's finest works in portraiture. She saw it at the Grosvenor Gallery's 1885 Winter Exhibition devoted to Gainsborough, a show which prompted more than usually severe criticism from her: '*The Blue Boy* is enough to immortalise any artist, but the common notion that a portrait or landscape being by Gainsborough must be valuable and excellent is completely erroneous. All great artists have painted rubbish at times, and Gainsborough ... has painted more than most'.

Given the importance of landscape as an ever-present background to her own work, it might be thought that Beatrix found inspiration in the landscapes of Gainsborough, which in some ways (such as misty distances or the formation of trees) have an affinity with hers. However, it is instructive to note that her inspiration in this field came not from Gainsborough but from Turner. On a dull November afternoon in 1884 in the basement of the National Gallery she and her father looked in awe at Turner's original landscape drawings for his collection of engravings published under the title of the *Liber Studiorum*. This single experience moved her to write: 'I think Turner is the greatest landscape painter that ever has lived, far superior to Claude or the Dutch painters'. Curiously enough, this was only her second visit to the National Gallery since she had once been there as a child, yet of all the paintings she had seen then, it was the Turners that had most stuck in her memory, above all his *Dido Building Carthage*. She returned to the Gallery later again that same month, and was even more enthusiastic. 'What marvellous pictures the Turners are! I think *Ulysses and Polyphemus* is the most wonderful in the Gallery.' One does not readily associate Beatrix with Turner at his most grandiose and dramatic.

To return to the Grosvenor Gallery: the point was made earlier that the Gallery provided a platform for artists of the day who were, it was felt, neglected or ignored by the Royal Academy. Amongst these were, for example, George Frederick Watts ('I believe he is all humbug, he draws shockingly [and] has hardly any colour.') and Lawrence Alma-Tadema, celebrated for his pictorial re-creations of life in Classical Greece and Rome, as well as for his industry. Indeed, so industrious was he that he was in grave danger of killing off the legendary golden-egg-laying goose. The effect on the public of an exhibition of his works held in 1885 was neatly summarised by Beatrix at the time: 'When [people] saw what a large number of Alma-Tademas there were in existence they don't like to give so much for a single one'.

Another regular exhibitor at the Grosvenor was the American-born painter James Abbot McNeill Whistler. Beatrix makes only one reference to him in her *Journal* (28 February 1883), but it is a highly significant one. 'Mr. Whistler is holding an exhibition somewhere, termed an *Arrangement in White and Yellow*. The furniture is painted yellow and the footman is dressed in white and yellow, someone said he looked like a poached egg. Mr. Whistler sent the Princess of Wales and the fine ladies yellow butterflies which they wore at the private view .... It's quite disgusting how people go on about these Pre-Raphaelite aesthetic painters.' There are several strands of information here which need to be separately unravelled.

Whistler was one of the most imaginative artists of his generation, and it was his habit to give his paintings unusual titles which emphasised his intense interest in colour and atmosphere. 'Arrangement' was a term which he used frequently: the famous portrait of his mother was originally called *Arrangement in Grey and Black*. Another favourite term was 'Nocturne'. Confronted in 1877 at the Grosvenor Gallery by a selection of Whistler's work including *Nocturne in Blue and Silver* (a mist-enshrouded evocation of old Battersea Bridge by moonlight), Ruskin in a famous phrase accused him of 'flinging a pot of paint in the public's face'. Whistler promptly sued for libel and was awarded a derisory farthing's damages.

Six years later he was still producing 'Arrangements', as Beatrix's comments show, but by then his poetic vision had become a part of the wider so-called Aesthetic Movement. Promoted by Whistler himself, by the poet Swinburne, by the art theorist Walter Pater, by the literary lion Oscar Wilde, and by their friends, the Aesthetic Movement spawned the doctrine of 'Art for Art's sake' and took itself very seriously. It inhabited a world whose epicentre was Kensington, whose living rooms were decorated with peacocks' feathers, artefacts from China and Japan, and furniture and textiles supplied by the firm of Morris and Co. The colour schemes of these rooms were novel, even startling, and took their cue from Morris, from Whistler, and from the Grosvenor Gallery itself. Here the walls of the main room were hung with panels of red silk, on which the paintings were displayed; beneath these the dado, from waist height down to skirting board level, was covered in green velvet, and it was this which, together with the extensive gilding, gave rise to the famous 'greenery-yallery' epithet so memorably used in 1884 by W.S. Gilbert in *Patience*:

A greenery-yallery,
Grosvenor Gallery,
Foot-in-the-grave young man.
This is how the poet Bunthorne describes himself, and indeed this languid character, lily in hand, is one of the best-known popular images of the entire Aesthetic Movement. Gilbert based him at least partly on Oscar Wilde, though by 1884 when Beatrix's parents saw him at a ball at Millais's house Wilde was anything but lanky and langorous; indeed he was (as she says) 'fat and merry'. She adds that, while he himself was not sporting a lily, 'his wife had her front covered in great water lilies'. The following year she saw him for herself and described him as 'rather a fine looking gentleman, but inclined to stoutness' (15 March 1885).

Sir Coutts Lindsay, the founder and proprietor of the Grosvenor Gallery, was a former military man as well as an artist; he in no way looked aesthetic and declared, 'I am not at all greenery-yallery either in feeling or anything else.' But the phrase stuck, and Beatrix herself uses it several times in her *Journal*. Robust as ever, she had little time for most of the contemporary artists who exhibited at the Grosvenor. After a visit there in July 1884, she wrote: 'As for the greenery yallery Grosvenor Gallery painters, they *is* there in full force, as contemptible as ever.' And when, later that same year, there was talk of the Gallery closing, she commented: 'What will become of the wretched greeneries I cannot imagine! They may well be more sickly than ever, for they have the prospect of extinction before them. I am sorry for them, but it is quite time they died.'

In general she was equally scornful of the Pre-Raphaelites, in whom, as a spin-off from the Aesthetic Movement, there was now a revival of interest, fuelled by the closely-related work of Edward Burne-Jones. Amongst Edward Crompton Potter's pictures there was, reported Beatrix, 'the un-avoidable Rossetti, ghastly and long-necked, with a trifle more work [in it] than usual.' Nevertheless it was on Rossetti's intense and brooding female images that the women of the Aesthetic Movement liked to model them-selves. According to Beatrix, Millais told her father that in his opinion Rossetti's pictures were rubbish and that Rossetti 'never learnt drawing and could not draw'. As the judgement of one former Pre-Raphaelite on another, this – as Beatrix herself noted – was rather odd, for Millais had been a founder member of the Pre-Raphaelite Brotherhood back in 1848, and naturally Beatrix excepted him from her generally poor opinion of Pre-Raphaelitism. Indeed, she felt (as is now generally believed) that much if not all of his best work was done as a Pre-Raphaelite, before he abandoned the Brotherhood's guiding principle of absolute truth to Nature and turned instead to the lucrative portrait-painting that was to make his later fame and fortune.

Christ in the House of His Parents by Sir John Everett Millais,
a close friend of the Potter family

Sometimes the pedantic naturalism of his Pre-Raphaelite phase was too much even for Beatrix; in *Christ in the House of His Parents* she found that '[his] endeavours to exactly copy Nature are painfully obvious'. But she thought his *Ophelia* 'probably one of the most marvellous pictures in the world', and she found *The Blind Girl* to be 'full of tender pathetic sentiment and painted in Millais's best style'.

She had also considerable admiration for Holman Hunt, both as a man and an artist. Hunt was famous for the amount of time he took to prepare a painting – years rather than months. This troubled Beatrix. 'His art cannot possibly repay the time spent on it,' she wrote. 'Whatever one may think of his work, one must respect the man, amongst the crowds of painters who dash off vulgar pictures to sell.' These comments were prompted by her first sight of Hunt's painting *The Triumph of the Innocents* (which she mistakenly calls *The Flight into Egypt*). This had taken him seven years to complete, more than two of which he had spent on site, as it were, in Jerusalem. Its appearance in 1885 at the Grosvenor Gallery caused, in Beatrix's words, 'a certain languid excitement'. She herself criticised the donkey and some of the children, as well as the colouring, but she was impressed by the composition and by the general idea behind the picture, which shows the Holy Family surrounded by the souls of the innocent children massacred by Herod.

In 1886 the Grosvenor put on a retrospective exhibition of Hunt's work, and here Beatrix's good opinions of him were reinforced. She especially

The Hireling Shepherd by William Holman Hunt

admired *The Hireling Shepherd* and *Strayed Sheep*; both of these convey a moral message cloaked in super-realism. Noting that many people took a violent dislike to his work, she wrote: 'I should have thought a man who could paint such pictures would be above caring for what the world says. He need not fear the future, real honest work will find its level in time, when the rubbish falls away and is forgotten.' When she also writes that 'There is much strong individuality and persistent self-reliance in his pictures', one can perhaps sense that here like was speaking to like.

Earlier, the *Innocents* had prompted another typical comment. Her father had complained that he couldn't understand the picture, to which she retorted that she would rather have such a picture than one which needed no understanding at all. But it was the Pre-Raphaelite paintings of Millais which inspired her to compose one of the briefest yet most succinct and penetrating evaluations of Pre-Raphaelite technique that has ever been produced. People often wonder what it is that gives Pre-Raphaelite paintings their almost unearthly brilliance and extreme clarity. Beatrix has the answer: 'Everything [is] in focus at once, which though natural in the different planes of the picture, produces on the whole a different impression from that which we receive from Nature.'

Her opinion of Burne-Jones is in stark contrast to all this. 'Dislike is a mild word for my feelings towards Burne Jones,' she wrote in 1884, and goes on to say that, but for the fact that he was being lauded in the press, 'he would be below contempt and notice'. His *King Cophetua and the Beggar Maid* was, she thought, some four hundred years out of date, finding that 'the figures are not over well drawn, the faces have no expression, [and] the beggar maid is of the

King Cophetua and the Beggar Maid
by Sir Edward Coley Burne-Jones

Love Locked Out by Anna Lea Merritt
with (below) the painting of Peter by the
locked door, from *The Tale of Peter Rabbit*

54

usual ugly type.' Elsewhere she criticises his work as being 'weak in drawing, morbid in style, and forced and ridiculous in sentiment'. She did, however, find some of his colour combinations harmonious, in particular the blues and greys, and she almost admired the stained glass which he designed for the windows of Christ Church Cathedral in Oxford. It is a pity that she knew nothing of the more human side of Burne-Jones as revealed in his painfully observant caricatures.

Beatrix Potter's own art is so intensely individual and personal that it is difficult to know how much, if at all, it benefited from her visits to the various exhibitions and permanent collections of paintings during these years. Where there is discernable influence, it is usually revealed in the form of parody, conscious or otherwise. Comparisons with the work of Rivière and Gainsborough have already been mentioned. There is also the now well-known correlation between Peter Rabbit standing forlornly outside the garden gate and the celebrated *Love Locked Out* by Anna Lee Merritt, painted in 1889. I should like to add here that Beatrix's study of Peter in queasy mood conveys, to me at least, faint echoes of portraits by Gainsborough or Reynolds, such as confronted her at the Royal Academy or Grosvenor Gallery.

But this is small beer. The real significance of Beatrix's artistic experiences in the 1880s and '90s lies in the trenchant comments and fearless criticism which they drew from her, as well as in the value which always attaches to the evidence of an independent observer.

Literature

The primary source for this and all similar studies relating to Beatrix Potter must of course be the *Journal*. Supplementary information has been obtained from the relevant exhibition catalogues of the Royal Academy and the Grosvenor Gallery. Mary Clive's book *The Day of Reckoning* (1964) gives a fascinating nursery-eye view of the kind of paintings that Beatrix saw (some of them the same ones). The Grosvenor Gallery and its founder Sir Coutts Lyndsay are dealt with by Virginia Surtees in her book *Coutts Lyndsay* (1993), and by Barrie Bullen in an article in the magazine *Apollo* for November 1975 (an issue devoted to the study of Burne-Jones and his period). Finally, nobody who is interested in Victorian painting should fail to read William Gaunt's two highly entertaining books, *The Aesthetic Adventure* (1945) and *Victorian Olympus* (1952).

Heck, Mell and Bink: Cross-passages between Lakeland Farmhouses and the American Colonies

VICTORIA SLOWE

THE PICTURESQUE Discovery of the Lakes and Mountains of Cumberland and Westmorland coincided, in the mid-eighteenth century, with the identification in the national consciousness of an unique place – the Lake District. That quality of uniqueness embraced a distinct unity of natural landscape and cultural scenery. Daniel Defoe and Celia Fiennes in the seventeenth century may have fretted over the poor, tumbledown dwellings of the native Cumbrians, but the Romantics of the eighteenth century saw them as homes fit for the Arcadian 'confraternity of shepherds', who epitomised the ideal oneness of man with Nature.

By no means all Cumbrians were part of the idyll. From the second quarter of the seventeenth century many left for the New World and the English-speaking colonies on the eastern coast of North America, either in search of a prosperous new life or freedom from religious persecution.

The two main ports dealing with this colonial trade were Lancaster and Whitehaven. The latter was favoured by George Washington's father and step-brother (natives of Appleby in Westmorland) and was targetted by John Paul Jones, the father of the American navy, during the War of Independence.

The settlers took some treasured possessions with them, of course, but, perhaps more importantly, they also took a treasury of accumulated cultural traditions, from floorplans and bank barns, to barn-raisings and reels, and including such thrifty crafts as rag rugs and patchwork.

Rag rugs, known in the Lake District as 'hookies and proddies', were made from outworn woollen material, cut into strips, which were literally hooked and prodded through coarse-woven sacking or canvas to create hard-wearing mats and rugs, whose abstract patterns enlivened earth, stone or wooden floors. Beatrix Potter had hookies and proddies on the floor at Hill Top:

several are depicted in *The Tale of Samuel Whiskers*. She also collected examples of that other craft connected with thrift and recycling: patchwork.

From the tone of her correspondence published in *Beatrix Potter's Americans: Selected Letters*, it is clear that Beatrix took great delight in the differences and similarities between the decorative arts of the Lake District and the American colonies which her transatlantic fans commented upon when she entertained them at Hill Top and Castle Cottage.

She was particularly interested in traditional oak furniture, always ready to buy prime examples at local sales in order to return them to their proper context in the Lakeland farmhouses from which they had been unceremoniously stripped. She also purchased those same farmhouses, eventually bequeathing them to the National Trust.

In April 1929, Beatrix Potter writes to Marian Frazer Harris Perry:

I saw you took notice of a fine carved chest in our dining room; it came out of 'Thimble Hall' [in Hawkshead; the exterior is illustrated in *The Fairy Caravan*]. I was sorry to move it; but the new tenant had children; and poor old Mrs Hunt who was leaving, begged me to take it away and take great care of it – poor old body; it had been in her mother's family, probably for hundreds of years; she said it would be sold when she died, and she 'might as well have the money', but she would not sell it to a stranger. There is a fine dated piece in another cottage belonging to me.

And on 13 December 1934, Beatrix Potter tells Bertha Mahony Miller:

The local furniture in this district was oak, rather out of fashion in the sale room now, but I collect any genuine pieces I can get hold of to put back into the farmhouses. The court cupboards with carved fronts are the most interesting as they are usually dated . . . . There are a good many in cottages belonging to the National Trust which will be preserved safely. The oldest I know is 1639.

A Romantic appreciation of Lakeland landscape and its traditional buildings – farmhouses, barns, shippons, walls, stiles and gateways – and their furnishings was strong in Beatrix Potter. Had her mentor, Canon H.D. Rawnsley pointed her towards Ruskin on *The Poetry of Architecture*? She certainly admired 'the mountain brotherhood' who knew how to build in keeping with their surroundings by instinct rather than design. The low whitewashed farmhouses with their round chimneys, massively built walls and lichened slates certainly look at home in their setting.

Why?

Such buildings are vernacular in quality, that is they are the product of local craftsmen meeting simple functional requirements according to traditional plans and procedures, and utilising local building materials and constructional methods. Although shelter was of far greater importance than aesthetic effect – if that were consciously considered at all – these 'statesmen' farmers and their neighbours had a natural eye for site and proportion and innate asymmetrical balance: their homes belong amongst the Lakeland fells and dales.

Most traditional Cumbrian farmhouses and their ancillary buildings date from 'The Great Rebuilding', which, in the north of England, where property was prey to the Border Reivers until the accession of James VI of Scotland to the English throne in 1603, took place from about 1610 until about 1760. Around the periphery of the Lake District, sandstone or gritstone or limestone door lintels bear carved dates and initials, but in the central fells, where the stone is not easily cut, the dates and initials are found on the oak panelling or built-in furniture inside. There are usually three initials: a large central one, representing the surname, flanked by two smaller ones standing for the forenames of husband and wife. The documentary evidence which survives suggests that the rebuilding usually coincided with a marriage or betrothal.

Sketch by Beatrix Potter of a three-tiered carved oak
cupboard or 'brideswain'

This is perhaps confirmed by the local name of 'brideswain' for the three-tiered built-in carved oak cupboards, (which are also known as 'bread cupboards', and which antique dealers call 'court cupboards'). These faced the main hearth: such cupboards, frequently decorated with variations of an interlocking double heart motif, were wedding presents and/or part of the bride's dowry.

Confirmation that this outbreak of constructional activity was, in fact, a *Rebuilding* comes from the mature character of the floorplan of the long-houses that were erected and from the re-use of such materials as cruck timbers, which were incorporated into the roof structures.

Such founders of the Cumberland and Westmorland Antiquarian and Archaeological Society as W.G. Collingwood and Henry Swainson Cowper were swift to identify the Lake District's Norse heritage in place-names, dialect, patronyms, legend, house-plans and carved motifs.

Beatrix Potter endorsed these views. She informs Marian Frazer Harris Perry, in a letter dated 25 April 1929:

The pronunciation of names is often a clue to their meaning; the natives call it 'Harksead' and 'Ammelsead' – Ambleside - which probably are Norse names, Haco seat, Hammel's seat; 'Saeter' is I believe still a Nor-wegian name for a farm steading.

And she had a pet theory that 'the craftsmen who carved our designs were imitating the runic interlacing. It would be too much to say that their patterns were developed from the Scandinavians because there is a complete gap between the early civilisation of High Furness and the return of prosperity after the Union .... I do not claim that the patterns are traditional; but I do think some one of the old joiners and carvers must have been familiar with such patterns as those on the Gosforth Cross.'

Archaeological field-work has still to prove the theories first voiced over a century ago, but received opinion agrees that the so-called 'Statesman Plan' (named after the form of customary tenure, inherited from father to son, which was the norm in the central Lakes), derives from the original Norse farmsteads established in the ninth and tenth centuries. The Norse long-houses had a central cross-passage providing access to the 'firehouse', with its focal hearth around which the people congregated and told their sagas, and to the unheated foodstore. Shelter for the livestock was built-on, in line. Such buildings were timber-framed, using a cruck construction technique: pairs of native sessile oak 'siles' supported a ridge beam and side purlins. This framework was covered with branches, thatched with heather, and finally laid with turf. The low walls were made of large boulders from becks and field clearance, consolidated with turf, but they carried no load.

THE STATESMAN PLAN
A Three Bay Farm House

Plan based on the
work of the late
Dr J. E. Partington,
Dr R. W. Brunskill
and
Dr W. Rollinson

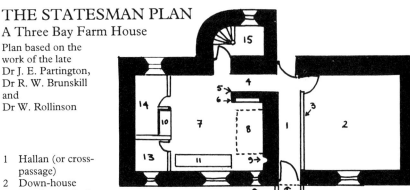

1 Hallan (or cross-passage)
2 Down-house
3 Wattle and daub partition
4 Mell
5 Heck
6 Sconce (or built-in bench/settle)
7 Fire-house (or house)
8 Hooded hearth
9 Spice cupboard
10 Brideswain (or bread cupboard)
11 Board
12 Firewindow (to light hearth)
13 Buttery (or dairy)
14 Chamber (or master's bedroom)
15 Spiral stair (stone or oak) to loft
16 Main entrance door, marked by sole or threshwood
17 Porch with binks

The 'Statesman Plan' of the seventeenth-century 'Great Rebuilding' features a central cross-passage, flagged and about four feet wide, which was known as the 'hallan'. The entrance doorway was marked by a board, about a foot high, which was known as the 'threshwood' (threshold) or 'sole', and was sheltered by a porch comprising two large flagstones, each hung at 45° from a central beam, with either supporting beams or dry-stone or flag walls, but no outer door. The porch contained at least one slate seat or shelf, known as a 'bink'. Beatrix Potter depicts a sophisticated version in *The Tale of The Pie*

Porch with a slate seat or shelf, known as a 'bink', from
The Tale of the Pie and the Patty-Pan

A sketch for Cecily Parsley brewing ale (or cider?), showing a 'down-house'

and The Patty-Pan, 'Duchess in the Porch' where Ribby's 'bink' is shown. The 'hallan' had one solid stone wall, and one of lath and plaster; at its far end were two facing doors. The door let into the lath and plaster wall opened into the 'down-house', the service area of the farm, used for washing, baking, brewing, pickling, spinning, and storing 'elding' (peat or wood fuel). Beatrix Potter set the illustration of 'Cecily Parsley makes Cowslip Wine', which replaced an earlier, banned version, 'Cecily Parsley brewing cider', in a typical 'down-house'. The 'down-house' was open to the rafters, and, in the late eighteenth and early nineteenth centuries, was often converted into the farm kitchen, first by the provision of an open hearth, and later by the installation of a cast-iron range, like those of Tabitha Twitchit, Ribby and Mr Tod. A smoking loft (for hams and mutton) was built above, together with accommodation for the female servants.

The opposite door, in the stone wall of the 'hallan', opened into a short and narrow passage, known as the 'mell', which led into the 'fire-house', the general living quarters. This was commonly known as the 'house', a variant of 'hearth and home', (in the phrase 'house and home'). The 'heck' partition, which formed the 'mell', was designed to protect the all-important hearth from draughts. The side of the 'heck' facing the fire incorporated a built-in bench or settle, known as the 'sconce', which was usually faced by the master's chair, a heavily carved, panelled status symbol. The children sat on three-legged stools, or 'coppies', which were also used for such tasks as milking: three legs were easier to balance than four on rough cobbles or flagstones. Recesses in the chimney wall held spices and the family Bible; the richer homes had plain, panelled or carved doors fitted over these recesses. A

61

'rannel balk' or chimney crane with 'rattan crooks' held the cooking utensils over the fire.

The nearest thing to a 'heck' and 'sconce' which Beatrix Potter drew is the settle occupied by the two clay-pipe-smoking, cider-drinking rabbits in 'Gentlemen came every day', which was given to Noel Moore, and later redrawn for the frontispiece of *Cecily Parsley's Nursery Rhymes*. Chimney (or fire) cranes with 'rattan crooks' (adjustable pot hangers) feature in 'Ready for the Party' in *The Tale of The Pie and The Patty-Pan*, in which Ribby is shown warming her paws at the grate. They also appear in 'Plenty of room for a little Tom Cat', in *The Tale of Samuel Whiskers* and in Mr Peter Thomas Piperson's fireplace, in front of which Pigling Bland sits on a 'coppy' in *The Tale of Pigling Bland*. Tom Kitten is shown 'balancing himself on the iron bar [rannel balk] where the kettle hangs' and taking 'another big jump off the bar' as he climbs the chimney in *The Tale of Samuel Whiskers*. The small, built-in, panelled wall cupboard which Duchess searches in the illustration 'Where is the pie made of mouse?' in *The Tale of The Pie and The Patty-Pan*, is a spice recess, with later door; the scene is lit by a small 'fire window', admitting daylight to the hearth area.

Beatrix Potter called the kitchen at Hill Top 'the hall', although she did use the term 'house-place', (a variant of 'fire-house') once or twice in her letters.

The hearth was the heart of the home, a veritable snug, where stories were passed down by word of mouth. The importance of fire and the strong oral tradition harks back to a Norse ancestry.

The pioneering antiquarians exploring folklore and survivals in the late nineteenth century, noted the preponderance of the hearth-cult and associated ancestor worship. In *The Village Community*, 1890, G.L. Gomme writes:

> An analysis of the customs which attended the primitive hearth-cult shows us that the sacred fire on the hearth was never allowed to go out; that the ritual attendant upon marriage, birth, and death, centred round the sacred fire; that offerings to the ancestral god at the hearth were made from the food of the household; and that the hearth represented to its early worshippers the source of all their happiness and prosperity.

Earlier, in 1864, in 'Hawkshead Town' (Transactions of the Lancashire & Cheshire Historic Society), A.C. Gibson had recorded an everlasting hearth-fire, as kept burning at the lonely farmsteads of Parkamoor and Lawson Park, on the moor between Hawkshead and Coniston Lake. Gibson comments:

> Previous to the invention of lucifer matches [an early form of safety match], and probably for long after, the fire on the stone hearths of these two 'Granges' had not been extinguished, it was said, for many centuries, probably not even yet. Their fuel being peat, was easily kept smouldering

Mary Ellen, the farm cat, seated by the hearth,
from *The Fairy Caravan*

throughout the longest night, while their distance from neighbours, and the consequent difficulty of providing means of re-lighting their fires, if extinguished, made their many generations of inmates careful to preserve them alight.

Beatrix Potter captures the significance of the hearth-cult in *The Fairy Caravan*, where the pen and ink drawing of 'Mary Ellen by the Fire' recalls a favourite drawing of her own cat, Thomasine, staring at the flames the day before she produced her seventh family. In a shadowy night scene, barely lit by the fire and the moon:

Mary Ellen, the farm cat, sat within; purring gently, and staring at the hot white ashes on the open hearth; wood ash that burns low, but never dies for years.

According to the local historian, Henry Swainson Cowper, in his book *Hawkshead* (1899):

In the same primitive stage of culture the foundation of the homestead was celebrated in more than one way, and of these the most important were sacrifice and feast. The latter still lingers in the 'rearing suppers', invariably given to the workmen by the master or employer on the day when the roof

Tom Kitten and the rats in the attic, showing the roof timbers
or 'cruck-blades', from *The Tale of Samuel Whiskers*

timbers are reared or raised into their place. The 'house warmings' of other parts have the same origin.

Such widespread traditions include the 'barn raisings' of North America, which possibly descend from the propitiatory offerings made after the matched pairs of siles in a Norse cruck barn had been hauled upright and into place.

In the Lakeland 'Statesman Plan' fire-house, and exactly opposite the hearth, which was usually lit by a small fire window, stood the already-mentioned 'brideswain', the three-tiered carved oak cupboard which was the most important symbol of wealth and prosperity. The 'brideswain' was built into a clam and daub partition, or sometimes into a stone wall, and, on either side of it, doors led into the 'chamber' (or best bedroom) and into the 'buttery', which was usually located on the northern side of the building for coolness. The earlier 'brideswains' had bulbous turned pillars to support the overhanging top tier, but later examples just have turned pendant drops.

Beatrix Potter was somewhat perplexed by the dates given by 'Mr Lockwood' in *Colonial Furniture*, a book sent to her in 1940 by Bertha Mahony Miller. Writing on 11 October 1940, Beatrix Potter comments:

The dates suggested by Mr Lockwood for oak furniture at first reading appear crazy? But upon reflection they are very interesting. The *patterns* are no guide to age where furniture is copied. For instance the 'press cupboards' with *pillars* supporting the canopy 'last quarter 17th century'. In this district if an old court cupboard built into the partition of an old farmhouse, has *pillars*, it is one of the earliest specimens. By the middle of the 17th cent., the pillars had become droppers. Many of the press cupboards illustrated are very beautiful, especially those with geometric panels and split-spindles – but they are obviously inspired by older designs than their American dates.

The friezes and panelled doors of the 'brideswain' provided plenty of scope for the local carver. The patterns found on such built-in furniture now help to identify the origins of portable items such as chairs and 'kists' (chests). Interlace patterns – geometrical, with foliate or dragonesque embellishment – are found throughout the Lake Counties, although the lozenge motif seems peculiar to Westmorland.

In the same letter to Bertha Mahony Miller, Beatrix Potter draws her favourite court cupboard:

It is very plain, except the middle, fixed panel, which has good carving. It will be noted that by 1667 *all* pillars had become droppers. We own only one cupboard – out of a dozen – which has pillars. It is built into a partition in a farmhouse at Wray near Ambleside. The cupboard shown above was detached when I bought it, in a farm sale in Cartmel near Kendal. But like all others now detached it had originally been a fixture. It is unusually long in shape. The 4 doors fasten with thumb pieces, and the doors hang on pins – i.e. iron rods instead of hinges.

She remarks:

It is a curious fact that cupboards and bible boxes very often have dates but chests almost never (unless the date is spurious). Many of the patterns in Mr Lockwood's book are like ours; for instance, the fleur-de-lys on the large board above.

Beatrix Potter was intrigued by comparing and contrasting the patterns carved on Furness/Westmorland and American oak. Her trained powers of observation and retentive visual memory, sharpened by a visit to Townend in Troutbeck, where 'Alas! old Miss Brown's [sic] old father was an enthusiastic carver in the bad Victorian days when amateurs "improved" old oak', provide the basis of further commentary:

In Mr Lockwood's photographs our most frequent design – foundations – occur, but our eight ∞ has turned into hearts in your patterns and his ⟨∿⟩ is foliated. I have a theory (only my own) that the craftsmen who carved our designs were imitating the runic interlacing . . . . I do not claim that the patterns are traditional; but I do think some one of the old joiners and carvers must have been familiar with such patterns as those on the Gosfirth [sic] Cross. Our figure of ⟨∞⟩ when elaborated is not a heart – it is ⟨⟳⟩ twists and in one of the panels of the Brown [sic] bedstead there is 'the worm Misgurd' clear enough (though to be sure he may be only an ordinary local adder) . . . . The next panel is a complicated strapwork *quite clearly* . . . . She has a livery cupboard, with spindles, unspoilt. Also a very fine table, with the original long benches beside it; one hinged to a wall and letting down, the other on legs . . . . I have a large chest that is interesting from having belonged to a well-known Ulverston family named Fell, iron masters . . . . This Ulverston chest has a running vine, a leaf-and-bunch-of-grapes design which occurs on Ulverston cupboards. I should be inclined to derive this pattern from the influence of Furness Abbey. I think it occurs on tiles.

The running vine motif features on the choir-stalls of Cartmel Priory, endorsing Beatrix Potter's opinion that it had monastic origins. The pattern features on at least one pair of bed posts from the Cark-in-Cartmel area: the bed into which the pair is incorporated is now in the Museum of Lakeland Life and Industry in Kendal.

I differ from Beatrix Potter over the heart motif, however, as numerous 'brideswains' in Hawkshead, Rusland and Langdale, as well as in North Westmorland, feature an interlocking double heart design, embellished by knots and spirals or by leaves and bracken fronds. Such a pattern endorses the local name of the cupboard – 'brideswain' – and links 'The Great Rebuilding' with family betrothals and weddings. Extant documentary evidence in family papers tends to confirm this.

In the closely-knit societies which existed in the Lakeland dales, 'bidden weddings' gave an opportunity for social contact, feasting and sports: the entire dale was 'lated' (invited) to a marriage. A fiddler led the couple to church, and afterwards the guests raced on foot (or on horseback) to the bridal house, where the victor received a riband from the bride. The celebrations included wrestling and leaping contests, foot races, and the strange custom of breaking the wedding cake (a thin, currant bridecake) over the bride's head. Later, the bride sat in state as the assembled guests placed money and other gifts in a plate on her knee. The final festivity was the time-honoured tradition of 'throwing the stocking' which is described thus by J. Hodgson in 'Westmorland As It Was', (reprinted in *The Lonsdale Magazine*, vol. 3, 1822):

a custom which refinement has proscribed as indelicate, though it offered no offence to the decorum of the rude simplicity of the people amongst whom it prevailed. It was, however, accessible only to a chosen party. While the new married couple sat upright in bed, with the curtains open only at the foot, the young men attempted to hit the bridegroom and the young women the bride, by throwing the bride's stockings over their shoulders. Those who were successful in the attempt went away assured that their marriage was near.

In such a robust and unpretentious age, the heart motif was the natural choice for the decoration of the furniture which was made for the couple's new home.

Beatrix Potter never attended a 'bidden wedding', of course, but in *The Lonely Hills* (*Horn Book*, May 1942) she reminisces over 'Merry Nights', remembering:

The stone-floored farm kitchen where first we danced 'The Boatman' and heard the swinging lilt of 'Black Nag'. The loft with two fiddles where country dancers paced 'The Triumph', three in arm under arched hands.

She remembers 'another unforgettable pageant' in Grasmere, surrounded by the fells:

The merry dancers! . . . a rainbow-hued kaleidoscope. In spite of roughish turf I have never seen . . . prouder beauty than the Durham reels danced by girls in corn-coloured smocks. The reels pleased me especially . . . . 'Three Reels', 'Petronella' and 'The Triumph' were traditional in this border country. My farm servants danced them at our Christmas suppers . . . give me the swinging, roaring, reels – the sparkling pretty long sets – the maze of intricate dances surprisingly remembered – follow the fiddle, forget your feet! Or dance with style and bend and sway; a bow and a curtsey for man and maid; and an inextricable tangle of laughter for beginners!

Had her American correspondents described square-dancing to Beatrix Potter? And had she pondered over its possible derivation from Cumbrian and Border reels?

The 'Statesman Plan' farmhouse's 'fire-house' contained the 'board' or table, which was, at first, literally a board set on three or more pairs of trestles. It was arranged parallel to the two mullion windows set in panelling which incorporated a built-in bench, and which, as at Townend, was often collapsible. Portable forms (benches) provided seating down the other length of the 'board'.

Access to the communal sleeping loft was gained by ladder, or, in richer homes, via a rough stone spiral stair built into – or out of – the chimney breast or accommodated into an apse-like, semi-circular bay on the outside wall.

A built-in window seat of the kind common in the 'Statesman Plan' farmhouse, from *The Tale of Mr Tod*

Some houses, particularly in market towns like Hawkshead, had outside stairs made of stone and slated, to the upper storey. Projecting eaves and jettied upper floors provided shelter for market goods from sun or rain; jettied floors provided more space at higher level, above laden-cart height, when taxable ground was at a premium. Open galleries at upper floor level provided connecting access from room to room, and a display area for goods, as well as shelter and storage space.

Around 1600, the richer homes gained more sophisticated oak staircases, at first dog-legged, then, from the mid-seventeenth century, more imposing, with panelling, hand-rail and turned banisters. At this stage, the loft was ceiled, and partitioned into dormitories for male and female children and servants. Walls were limewashed. By the eighteenth century, colour was being added by the judicious use of damson juice (pink), rudd or ruddle (coral), or, later in the nineteenth century, dolly blue.

Externally, the seventeenth-century buildings were enlivened by slate drip-courses over the windows and the junction between chimney and roof. As quarrying and mining rights fell into secular hands for commercial exploitation, thatch was replaced by slated roofs. Early slates are thicker and rougher than modern ones, and were pegged in place with timber dowels or sheep bones. There was no suitable free stone in the central fells from which to make ridge tiles to waterproof the join at the apex of the roof, but the problem was resolved through the invention of 'wrestler' or 'wrassler' slates, which were cut into a T-shape so that the arms of the 'T' interlocked, from opposite sides of the roof, along the ridge. Fine examples can be seen on The Bridge House, Ambleside.

Chimneys were frequently constructed in a cylindrical form, rising from a square base, and topped by slates and stones to control the draught. Wordsworth was one of the first local writers to praise the vernacular buildings:

> Among the numerous recesses and projections in the walls and in the different stages of their roofs, are seen bold and harmonious effects of contrasted sunshine and shadow .... Sometimes a low chimney, almost upon a level with the roof, is overlaid with a slate supported upon four slender pillars.

He also extolled the 'vegetable furniture' of fern, moss and lichen advocated by the Rev. William Gilpin in his *Observations on the Mountains and Lakes of Cumberland and Westmorland*, 1772.

Window surrounds were whitened to reflect light into the dark, oak-panelled rooms, but limewashing the whole of the exterior walls of the farmhouse did not come into fashion until the last quarter of the eighteenth century. Wordsworth reviled this change which he felt made the farmhouses stand out too obviously against the surrounding fields and fells, although, conversely, he admired Hawkshead Church, which was roughcast outside and whitewashed until 1875. The poet recalls his return to Hawkshead (where he had attended the grammar school) at the end of his first year at Cambridge, in the summer of 1788, in *The Prelude*:

> I saw the snow-white church upon her hill
> Sit like a throned lady sending out
> A gracious look all over her domain.

Rough-casting and lime-washing the exterior was, like oak-panelling the interior, an effective way of draught-proofing dry-stone walls which, as the name suggests, were constructed without mortar.

The oldest surviving farm buildings, dating from the seventeenth century, are built on the bank-barn principle, against and into the hillside; shippons or stables are located at the lower level, with a penthouse roof providing shelter over the doors. At the upper level, large double doors, reached by a ramp, open on to a stone threshing floor, with a small winnowing door opposite to create a wind-tunnel effect when 'deeting' grain, to separate (in this northern clime) the oat from the chaff. The shallow sheepskin dish used in 'deeting' or winnowing grain was known as a 'weyt': the 'weyt' also had a festive use, as a drum to sound the rhythmic beat for reels and dances.

Galleries, under penthouse roofs, provided protected exterior passages

A sketch for Lucie's 'farm called Little-town' – actually Skelgill near Gutherscale – showing the exterior of a farmhouse and a bank-barn, from *The Tale of Mrs Tiggy-Winkle*

and landings linking various sections of the building and providing additional, sheltered storage and work space. An attractive bank-barn, built by the Browne family, is still in use at Townend, Troutbeck.

Bank-barns are found in many hilly parts of the world from the Yorkshire Dales to Norway, from Switzerland to Pennysylvania and Ohio, and West Virginia. Does the design solution of the 'bank-barn' evolve naturally, from the lie of the land? Or did the idea cross the Atlantic from the Old World to the New, with the settlers?

Origins intrigued Beatrix Potter. She was fascinated not by family in the hierarchical sense of distinguished lineage, but by the influence of cultural and historic 'roots'. The first and most important essay which Beatrix Potter wrote about her work was published in *The Horn Book* in May 1929 in response to a request from the editor, Bertha Mahony Miller, for biographical and literary information. Long before Arthur Hailey made the topic fashionable, Beatrix Potter stated:

The question of 'roots' interests me! I am a believer in 'breed'; I hold that a strongly marked personality can influence descendants for generations. In the same way that we farmers know that certain sires – bulls – stallions –

rams – have been 'prepotent' in forming breeds of shorthorns, thorough-breds, and the numerous varieties of sheep. I am descended from generations of Lancashire yeomen and weavers; obstinate, hard-headed, *matter of fact* folk. (There you find the down-right matter-of-factness which imports an air of reality.) As far back as I can go, they were Puritans, Nonjurors, Nonconformists, Dissenters. Your *Mayflower* ancestors sailed to America; mine at the same date were sticking it out at home; probably rather enjoying persecution. The most remarkable old 'character' amongst my ancestors – old Abraham Crompton, who sprang from mid-Lancash-ire, bought land for pleasure in the Lake District; and his descendants seem to have drifted back at intervals ever since – though none of us own any of the land that belonged to old Abraham.'

In other words, the genes will out – in the Herdwick, in the native Fell pony which descends from the Frisian horses which the Frisian Legion rode along Hadrian's Wall, in the Lakeland dalesmen and Statesmen farmers who have Norse blood in their veins and in the common cultural heritage of the early American settlers.

The traditional farmhouses of the Lake District are the happy result of nature and nurture, of environment and genes. Very well-planned and designed to suit the terrain, building sites, locally available materials, and the needs and heritage of the occupants, their genesis and evolution over nearly a millennium goes much of the way towards explaining just why they suit their setting so well – and also the timelessness of their universal appeal.

Architectural fads and fashions come and go, but inherent style remains for ever. Beatrix Potter recognised this, celebrating the exteriors and interiors of the picturesque Lakeland farmhouses in both the text and the illustrations of her 'little books', and ensuring the survival, in perpetuity, of some of her favourite examples by bequeathing them to the National Trust.

Bibliography

Life and Tradition in the Lake District, William Rollinson. J.M. Dent & Sons, London, 1974

Vernacular Architecture of the Lake Counties, R.W. Brunskill. Faber & Faber, London, 1974

Beatrix Potter's Americans: Selected Letters. Edited by Jane Crowell Morse. Horn Book, Boston, Mass., 1982

Beatrix Potter 1866–1943: The Artist and her World, Judy Taylor, Joyce Irene Whalley, Anne Stevenson Hobbs, Elizabeth M. Battrick. F. Warne & Co. and The National Trust, 1987

Hawkshead: its History, Archaeology, Industries, Folklore, Dialect, etc, Henry Swainson Cowper. Bemrose & Sons Ltd, London & Derby, 1899.

The Humour of Beatrix Potter

SELWYN GOODACRE

I DON'T THINK many of us immediately think of Beatrix Potter as a humorous woman. Quite the opposite – especially when we look at those photographs of her clomping around northern agricultural shows in those frightful clogs and ill-fitting Herdwick wool clothes, or recall anecdotes of her shouting at local village children who trespassed on her land. And yet there is no doubt whatsoever that she did have a keen sense of humour and a heightened appreciation of the absurd.

Analysing humour is beset by many obstacles. Humour tends to run along national lines – and personal lines. A sense of humour is very individual. I personally may find Tommy Cooper, or Morecambe and Wise the funniest stand-up comedians, or consider *Cold Comfort Farm* to be the funniest book ever written – but others may have quite different opinions. English people never find Bob Hope as funny as the Americans do. By all accounts the sexist humour of Benny Hill is enjoyed more by American than by English audiences. Western eyes wonder why the Japanese find those strange TV endurance games shows so terribly amusing.

So, when we consider what Beatrix Potter found amusing, we do not necessarily have to agree, nor should we necessarily expect to share her perceptions ourselves. I read through her complete *Journal* in preparation for my talk at the Conference (and learnt a lot more than I ever wanted to, about nineteenth-century politics, and the paintings in the National Gallery), and was struck by the number of anecdotes she records. Presumably she quotes them either from the family daily paper, or from a periodical like *Punch*. The anecdotes tend to be more in evidence in the earlier years of the *Journal*. Possibly she grew less fond of them as the years went by. Certainly Beatrix seems to have found them amusing at the time, and worthy of preservation. To our eyes they may appear a little dated:

Here lies Old Jones, who all his life collected bones - till death that grim and

72

bony spectre – that all amazing bone collector – bound old Jones so neat and tidy – so there he lies all bone fide.

A worthy missionary who had just returned from the South Seas was asked by a friend 'how he liked babies?' 'Boiled,' replied the missionary.

The Queen talking to Earl Aberdeen 'I have heard you are never sea-sick, Earl Aberdeen?'; 'Always, madam', 'But not very?' 'Very madam.'

They may evoke in us a slight smile, but they don't make us guffaw, but then why should they? Reading any Victorian issue of *Punch* can be a dispiriting experience, as some types of humour date easily, though really great humour is universal. The humour in sections of *The Pickwick Papers* by Charles Dickens, or in Jerome K. Jerome's *Three Men in a Boat* is timeless.

Rather than the anecdotes, I would suggest we are more in sympathy with those occasional lovely turns of phrase, the juxtaposition of disparate ideas, and Beatrix's little ironic remarks – all of which combine to give us clear evidence of a more personal underlying humour:

22 February 1883. Have had a cold most of the time since Christmas, have almost had enough of it. Think it's going to stop till Easter.

6 March 1883. Bought a wild duck Sat 10th. Mr Phillips said it would keep for three weeks. Could not help wondering if he knew from experience.

28 March 1884. It seems doubtful how the Queen will stand the death of her favourite son. No one says much of it, but for some months it has been suspected that all is not right with her. Some say she is mad, not that that is anything uncommon, half the world is mad when you come to enquire.

24 April 1884 [of a local earthquake]. I wish I had been in London to feel it *slightly.* One does not often get a chance of feeling an earthquake fortunately, in nature that is to say, for domestic ones are only too frequent.

There is an almost Woodhousian use of the unusual simile:

19 November 1884 [concerning a Mr Cutter, owner of a shop near the British Museum]. Old and musty from head to foot, with spectacles, he moved about among the piled-up lumber and curiosities and old bones of his shop like a wood-louse diving in and out of a rotten log.

1 February 1886. The butler hurried up the steep staircase like a beetle.

Her early powers of observation produce wonderfully vivid descriptions of curious personalities:

11 September 1892. Perched just below him … is the Precentor, a fine big

Charlie McIntosh, the Dunkeld postman and expert on fungi, c.1880

man with a bullet head, chubby red face, retroussé nose and a voice like a bull.

And of the great Charlie McIntosh:

I asked him to sit down, his head being somewhere in the chandelier. I would not make fun of him for the world, but he reminded me so much of a damaged lamp post.

We savour the nicely clipped opinions:

7 October 1892. News in *The Scotsman* of Lord Tennyson's death, a truly great patriot when treason is little thought of. What a pity it was not Mr Gladstone.

Writing as a family doctor, I find Beatrix's attitude to death delightfully refreshing. Let us leap forward in time, for a moment, to 18 December 1932:

My old mother is refusing to die. She was unconscious for 4 hours yesterday, and then suddenly asked for tea. She cannot possibly recover.

Sometimes death is reduced to an amusing anecdote:

13 January 1885 [concerning a correspondence in *The Times* about fire-arms]. A shocking example has lately occurred at Huddersfield, where an unfortunate gentleman thinking he heard burglars in the middle of the night, went downstairs and shot his cook dead.

7 January 1896. [An old lady left] twenty-five guineas by her will, and directions that her coffin should have a glass lid, and that he should look at her every morning for a fortnight. He said she did not improve, but seemed to consider it not an unpleasant way of earning his legacy. He just looked in every morning and there was no doubt that she was dead!

There is a delightful lengthy account of a visit to her 'Aunt Sidney', with whom she felt a great affinity. Beatrix comments on the Aunt's 'sense of humour' – 'evident in everything she says, but how seldom do we see humour joined with so tender a sympathy with the sadder and graver side of life.' This is a highly significant remark. Beatrix values humour in a most positive way, she views it as complementary to sadness and the serious side of life, and as a fundamental element in all aspects of life, however serious. Deeply serious people are often the most amusing.

Much of her best humour comes from a close observation of life, and with a precise and skilful use of the right phrase – this was of course to come to brilliant fruition in the little books. But we catch prescient glimpses in the *Journal*:

27 July 1892. Scotch papers are refreshingly acrimonious and spiteful provided you agree with them.

19 April 1895. I fell over a certain camera of papa's which I opportunely broke, a most inconveniently heavy article which he refuses to use, and which has been breaking my back since I took to that profession.

April 1895. I do not often consider the stars, they give me a tissick. It is more than enough that there should be 40,000 named and classified funguses.

I have commented on the occasional Woodhousian turn of phrase. On one occasion, she even gives us a foresight of J.P. Salinger in *The Catcher in the Rye*. Holden, you may recall, refers to a friend, whose mother had said he was very sensitive, as being – 'about as sensitive as a goddam toilet seat'. Beatrix on 8 August 1895 writes, 'Miss Gentile has as much sentiment as a broom-stick'.

Occasionally we find just what makes Beatrix actually laugh out loud – and it is hardly the thing one would expect. A curious example occurred during a

Beatrix Potter photographed by her father Rupert outside Kent's Cavern,
which they visited during a holiday at Torquay in Devon.

guided tour of a cave near Torquay. A group of people came into the cave 'a lady and some children and a spaniel like *Spot*'. Apparently it was the behaviour of the dog sneezing in a distant section of the cave that so amused her: 'I don't know when I laughed so.'

That she thought seriously about the merits of humour in good literature comes out when she is discussing old novels. She speaks disparagingly of *The Curse of Kehama*, because it is 'utterly devoid of the absurd'.

And so to the 'little books'. Curiously I have never found the one book which I think she intended to be funny – *The Tale of The Pie and The Patty-Pan* – particularly funny myself. Everybody thinks of this book as the 'Funny Potter book'. Until this Conference, I had a problem with it. I found it laboured, and unconvincing – perhaps I took subconscious offence at the portrait of the utterly incompetent country GP – the unflatteringly named Dr Maggotty, whose vocabulary is restricted to Gammon, Spinach, and Ha Ha. Happily my problem was solved at the Conference by a brilliantly humorous public reading of the whole book by Veronica Hickie. And yes, it is a wonderfully humorous portrayal of the social niceties of the time, as satirised in the small town society life of Duchess and Ribby.

It is an interesting exercise to ask: 'Which do you consider to be the books that contain the funniest episodes?' I would suggest three to you. The first is *The Tale of The Flopsy Bunnies*. I am on record as calling this little book Beatrix Potter's masterpiece – consider, for instance, that lovely description of the family: 'They had a large family, and they were very improvident and cheerful.'

Thomasina Tittlemouse bumps into the sleepy Benjamin Bunny. 'She rustled across the paper bag, and awakened Benjamin Bunny.

The mouse apologised profusely, and said that she knew Peter Rabbit.'

We chuckle at the brilliant juxtaposition of 'improvident' and 'cheerful', and enjoy the way the multisyllabic 'apologised profusely' is followed by the monosyllabic phrase.

My second choice is *The Tale of Tom Kitten*. Surely the high point in this charming book is the beautiful account of Mrs Tabitha Twitchit – only a deeply humorous person could make up such a brilliantly funny, and yet exactly right name, and then let everything she says be so perfectly and delightfully and humorously exactly right:

She pulled them off the wall, smacked them, and took them back to the house.

'My friends will arrive in a minute, and you are not fit to be seen; I am affronted,' said Mrs Tabitha Twitchit.

Somehow there were very extraordinary noises over-head, which disturbed the dignity and repose of the tea-party.

'She pulled them off the wall, smacked them, and took them back to the house', from *The Tale of Tom Kitten*

'I cannot bear ... to see them going out at the door carrying their little parcels', from *The Tale of Ginger and Pickles*

The ironic and serious phrases with the long vowels wonderfully enhance the basic humour of the situation.

And finally I choose *The Tale of Ginger and Pickles*. We have here a prime example of Beatrix's use of ironic humour - where Ginger requests Pickles to serve the mice–

'I cannot bear ... to see them going out at the door carrying their little parcels'.

This statement is totally belied by the picture on the facing page, which shows him nearly falling over the counter in his efforts to see them going out of the door.

We all know the quality of the little books. Humourous touches are everywhere, though particular sections will appeal to some more than to others. Some will delight in the goings on between Tommy Brock and Mr Tod, some may even laugh out loud at Pigling Bland, though I am not of that number. For examples of more obvious humour may I commend the wonderful miniature letters. They give us delightfully humorous insights into certain aspects of their books of origin

Master P Rabbit,
Under Fir Tree

Sir,
I rite by desir of my Husband Mr McGregor who is in Bedd with a Cauld to say if you Comes heer agane we will inform the Polisse
Jane McGregor

P.S. I have bort a new py-Dish, itt is vary Large.

and Peter's response

Master Benjamin Bunny,
The Warren.

Dear Cousin Benjamin,
I have had a very ill written letter from Mrs McGregor she says Mr M is in bed with a cold will you meet me at the corner of the wood near their garden at 6 this evening? In haste
Yr. Aff. Cousin,
Peter Rabbit.

You will remember other letters: Nutkin trying to get his tail back, and the unnamed Flopsy Bunnies, each writing their own little letters.

In spite of, or perhaps because of, her strange upbringing, Beatrix Potter developed a fierce independence of spirit. She viewed all experiences positively, and in spite of a morose, gloomy and selfish mother, and a seemingly humourless father, maintained a fine self-knowledge, and an independent and unique sense of humour, which began to emerge in the pages of her *Journal*, and which enhanced and supported many elements in her creative writing, and particularly in her books for children.

I commend her highly.

An illustration for the privately printed
edition of *The Tale of Peter Rabbit*. The
picture of Mrs McGregor and the pie
was omitted from later editions.

The Beatrix Potter Society

The Beatrix Potter Society was founded in 1980 by a group of people professionally involved in the curatorship of Beatrix Potter material. It exists to promote the study and appreciation of the life and works of Beatrix Potter (1866-1943), who was not only the author and illustrator of *The Tale of Peter Rabbit* and other classics of children's literature, but also a Natural History artist, diarist, farmer and conservationist – in the latter capacity she was responsible for the preservation of large areas of the Lake District through her gifts to the National Trust.

The Society is a registered charity and its membership is worldwide. Its activities include regular talks and meetings in London and visits to places connected with Beatrix Potter. An annual Linder Memorial Lecture is given each spring to commemorate the contribution made to Beatrix Potter studies by Leslie Linder and his sister Enid. The first of these was given at the Victoria and Albert Museum by Margaret Lane, as Patron of the Society. Biennial Study Conferences are held in the Lake District and Scotland and are attended by members from around the world.

A quarterly Newsletter, issued free to members, contains articles on a wide range of topics as well as information about meetings and visits, reviews of books and exhibitions, members' letters, and news of Beatrix Potter collections both in the United Kingdom and elsewhere. The Society also publishes the proceedings of its Study Conferences and various occasional papers.

For further information write to: The Membership Secretary, High Banks, Stoneborough Lane, Budleigh Salterton, Devon, EX9 6HL.